Deerfoot in The Mountains

Deerfoot in The Mountains

by Edward Sylvester Ellis

CHAPTER I.

EASTWARD BOUND.

Deerfoot the Shawanoe, Mul-tal-la the Blackfoot, and the twin brothers, George and Victor Shelton, had completed their long journey from the Ohio River to the Pacific slope, and, standing on an elevation near the Columbia, spent hours in looking out upon the face of the mightiest ocean of the globe. They feasted their vision on the magnificent scene, with the miles of wilderness, mountain, vale, river and Indian villages spread between their feet and the ocean.

It was a picture worth journeying across the continent to see. From beyond the convex world a ship had sailed up to view, its snowy sails looking at first like a tiny but growing cloud in the soft sky. As the craft drew steadily nearer, they saw it careening to one side under the impulse of the wind against the bellying canvas, while the curling foam at the bows spread out like a fan and dissolved in the clear waters beyond the stern.

Deerfoot had taken the glass after Mul-tal-la was through, and he stood for a long time gazing at the waste of waters. None spoke, for there was that in the scene and the occasion which made all thoughtful. The grandeur, the majesty, the vastness filled them with awe and held them mute. Finally, the Shawanoe lowered the instrument, and turning toward the boys, said gravely, as he pointed first to the east and then to the west:

"Yonder is the endless forest of wood, and yonder the endless forest of water; they shall all become the home of the white man."

"I don't doubt you are right," replied George Shelton, "but it will be hundreds of years after you and I are dead; there is room between here and the Ohio for millions upon millions, but where will they come from?"

"The white men will become like the leaves in the forest and the sands on the seashore; no one can count the numbers that will overspread the land; they will be everywhere."

"And what of your own people, Deerfoot?" asked Victor.

The dusky youth shook his head, as if the problem was beyond him.

"The two ought to live in peace side by side, for such is the will of the Great Spirit. The white man cannot become like the red man, but the red man may grow into the ways of the pale-faces, and all may be brothers, and so live till time shall be no more."

The theme was too profound for the youths, though it was manifest that the Shawanoe had given much thought to it. He added nothing, and while the day was young they walked back to the Columbia, re-entered the canoe and headed up stream.

Henceforward their work was different from that which they faced when descending the river. There were long stretches where, despite the current, the dusky boatmen found no special trouble in driving the craft eastward; but, as they progressed, the labor became severer, for the stream narrowed and the velocity of its flow became greater. The portages were long and toilsome, and, as the party advanced, many places were met where these portages became necessary on account of the rapidity of the current alone. All, however, bent resolutely to work, Victor and George taxing their strength to the utmost. Deerfoot seemed tireless, but he could never be inconsiderate to others. He could have outworn Mul-tal-la, though not till after the exhaustion of the boys, who agreed between themselves that the job was the biggest they had ever tackled; and yet their adult companions not only did the work the twins were doing, but swung the paddles in addition.

Our friends stayed one night at the Echeloot or Upper Chinook village, which they had visited when coming down the river. You will remember that it was there they first saw wooden houses made by Indians. The explorers were treated as hospitably as before, but, as you will also recall, the natives were Flatheads, and the sight of the misshapen skulls, towering at the rear like the ridge of a roof, was so disagreeable that the travelers were glad to turn their backs upon them.

You have not forgotten the thrilling descent of the Falls of the Columbia, where all the skill of Deerfoot and Mul-tal-la was needed to save the canoe from being dashed upon the rocks.

"Are you going to paddle through them again?" asked Victor.

"Deerfoot does not wish to see his brother scared so bad as he was before."

"I was about to say that if you and Mul-tal-la don't feel equal to the task, George and I are ready to take it off your hands."

"The heart of Deerfoot is made glad to hear the words of his brother," replied the Shawanoe, handing his paddle to the youth. Not expecting that, Victor scratched his head and looked quizzically at George.

"Shall we show those fellows how to do such things?"

"I don't think it is worth while; they won't appreciate it."

"Deerfoot is sorry," was all that was said by the Shawanoe, as the boat was drawn out of the waters and hoisted upon the shoulders of the party.

The Shawanoe gave another illustration of his stern principles when, at the close of day, the canoe was run into shore at the point where the travelers had encamped beside the pile of lumber from which they were led to take what fuel they needed through the misrepresentation of the three Indians who called upon them. The night was one of the coldest of several weeks, and at their elbows, as may be said, was enough fuel to make them comfortable for months.

The brothers looked longingly at the mass of lumber, but did not dare touch it in the presence of their friend.

"I wonder if we can't persuade him to look the other way for a little while," said Victor in a low tone to George.

"It wouldn't make any difference if he did—he would see us just the same; the only thing to do is to appeal to his common sense."

"You try it; he won't pay any attention to me."

"See here," said the shivering lad; "it seems to me, Deerfoot, that since we have already stolen some lumber from that pile, it can't be any harm to steal a little more; you see, with your good sense, that it will be only taking two bites from the same apple."

The Shawanoe looked gravely at his young friends, whom no one understood better than he, and abruptly asked:

"How much do two and two make?"

"As near as I can figure out," interposed Victor, "the answer to that problem is four."

"When we used the wood we thought we had the right to take it; we should pay the owner if we could find him. If we use any of it now it will be a sin, as sure as two and two make four, for we know it belongs to another; it is better to freeze than to steal wood. Deerfoot does not wish to hear his brothers say anything more."

"I suppose he is right," growled Victor, "but doesn't he draw it mighty fine? We may as well prepare to spend one of the worst nights we have had since leaving the Ohio."

The canoe was drawn up the bank and then turned over, so as to shield the property beneath. Then the blankets were spread so that the four lay near one another and thus secured mutual warmth. The region had become familiar to our friends because of their former visit, and they knew that all the natives were friendly. Deerfoot, therefore, said there was no need of mounting guard. They had eaten enough dried salmon to stay the pangs of hunger, though the boys would have relished something warm and more palatable.

All slept soundly, and the night passed without the slightest disturbance from prowling man or animal. Victor Shelton was the first to awake. He was lying on his side with his back against that of his brother, and his face so covered by his blanket that only a small orifice was left through which to breathe. His first sensation was that of pressure, as if a heavy weight was distributed over the blanket and was bearing him down. He moved his arm and found that the blanket, from some cause, was really heavier than usual. A vigorous flirt freed his shoulder from the wrapping, and he then saw the cause of the peculiar feeling he had noticed: the earth was covered with several inches of snow. Anyone coming upon the camp in the gray light of morning would have noted nothing but the mass of lumber, the flowing river, the overturned canoe and several white mounds. The snowfall had ceased, and fortunately there had been a considerable rise of temperature. The snow was soft and wet, and one could move about without extra protection, and not suffer from cold.

Victor lay still for a minute or two, engaged in thinking. Then he gently pushed the blanket off his shoulder and body, so as to leave his limbs free. With the same stealth he rose to his feet and looked around. There lay his three friends, encased even to their heads and feet in the warm protection.

"I think there couldn't be a better time for me to settle my accounts with you fellows," muttered the lad, looking down on the mounds.

"Master George Shelton, you have a bad habit of making slurring remarks about my walking pretty fast from the wounded antelope, forgetting that by doing so I drew him on to his own destruction. You need a lesson and I'm going to give it to you.

"Mr. Mul-tal-la, you didn't say much at the time I was explaining that little matter to George, but I saw the grin on your face, and I knew you were thinking a good deal more than you had any right to think. You need to be taught better manners.

"As for you, Mr. Deerfoot, you are the worst of all. I can't forget the scandalous tricks you have played on me. It will take a long time to even matters between us, but I'm going to make a good start to-day."

Knowing how lightly the Shawanoe slept, Victor picked his way with great skill until he had taken a dozen or more steps. The down-like carpet enabled him to do this absolutely without noise, a fact which explains why Deerfoot did not awake.

Victor now stooped and began silently manufacturing snowballs. He packed the soft substance as hard as he could while circling it about in his palms and rounding it into shape. When the missile suggested a 12-pound shot he laid it at his feet, with the whispered words:

"That's for you, Master George Shelton."

The second sphere was compressed and modeled with the same pains and placed beside the first.

"That's for you, Mr. Mul-tal-la, and you're going to get it good! As for you, Mr. Deerfoot, you shall have a double dose."

Crooking his left arm at the elbow, Victor laid three of the nicely molded snowballs in the hollow, which served as a quiver serves for arrows. The fourth missile was grasped in his right hand, and he drew it slowly back and sighted carefully at his brother. Victor was a fine thrower, and when the ball flashed from his hand it landed on the top of George's cap and burst into fragments. The sleeper was in the midst of a dream in which Zigzag played a leading part, and the youth's first impression was that he had received the full force of a kick on his crown.

Paying no further attention to him, Victor quickly let fly at Mul-tal-la, and the throw was as good as the first.

The disturbance, slight as it was, roused Deerfoot, who flung the blanket off his face and raised his head. He was just in time to receive the compact sphere between the eyes, and before he could dodge the second it landed on his ear, packed the passage full of snow and plastered the side of his face with the snowy particles.

"I meant those for you and here's another!" shouted Victor, who, having exhausted his ammunition, snatched up a handful of snow and began hastily molding a new missile.

"You needn't scramble and claw about! I've got you down and I'm going to pay you for beating me at wrestling, for tickling my nose, for stealing my clothes when I was swimming, and"——

The reason why the lad ceased his remarks so abruptly was because a snowball, fired as if from a cannon, crashed into his mouth that instant and half strangled him. Before he could pull himself together he knew his nose was flattened by another missile and Deerfoot was on the point of launching a third shot. This was more than Victor had bargained for, and, wheeling, he "ran for life," yelling at the top of his voice for George and Mul-tal-la to come to his help.

"Soak him, George! Give it to him, Mul-tal-la; don't you see he's killing me?"

Now, there was no reason why the two thus appealed to should heed the prayer, since each had suffered at the hands of the youth who was in extremity. Nevertheless, Mul-tal-la and George attacked Deerfoot, observing which, Victor was unprincipled enough to turn back and join the assailants. Thus the Shawanoe was forced to defend himself against three, every one of whom was a good thrower. Right bravely did the dusky youth do his work—never yielding an inch, but driving his missiles right and left, with the merciless accuracy and the power of an arrow from his bow, or a bullet from his rifle. So lightning-like were his throws that neither the man nor the boys were able to dodge them, unless they widened the space between themselves and their master. Deerfoot's last missile cracked like a pistol when the ball impinged against the side of Mul-tal-la's head, and the latter gave up the contest.

This left only the boys. The Shawanoe hastily fashioned a couple of balls, and with one in either hand started for the brothers, who called out, "Enough!" and flung their own ammunition to the ground in token of surrender. He looked from one to the other and said:

"Let us not stop; Deerfoot is beginning to like it."

"That's the trouble," replied George; "you like it too much; I don't want any more; maybe Victor does."

"I'll do my own talking," replied the latter; "didn't you see me throw down my snowball? What do you 'spose I did that for?"

"Didn't you throw it at Deerfoot?" asked the Shawanoe. "The shot came as near hitting him as some of those you threw."

"We'll take up the fight again some time," was the vague promise of Victor, panting from his exertion.

"Deerfoot hopes you will do so."

But the good-natured contest was never renewed. Not again could the lads expect to have such a golden opportunity, and their defeat was so decisive that they knew better than to repeat it.

The labor of the return grew heavier as they progressed, and the time came when it was so hard to make headway against the powerful current that the effort was given up. The last few miles became a real portage, though when our friends were descending the river the passage could not have been easier.

And so in due time the four reached the Nez Perce village, where they had left their horses and some of their property. Henceforth the journey to the Blackfoot country was to be made by land. The former task had proved one of the severest of their lives, and glad indeed were all when it was over.

CHAPTER II.
LOST, STRAYED OR STOLEN.

You have already learned something of the Nez Perces, who in our times have produced one of the greatest Indian leaders of the past century. He was Chief Joseph, who gave the United States regulars such a brilliant campaign as to excite their admiration. Perhaps you saw the aged chief on his visit to the East a short time since. He was chivalrous, high-minded and a loyal friend of the whites, and showed this when he handed his rifle to Colonel Miles and said: "From where the sun stands in yonder heavens, I fight the white man no more."

You will recall that the Nez Perces are large, fine-looking men, of dark complexion, and that the women have attractive features. A century ago they had a rough time of it. They were forced to work hard during the summer and autumn in gathering salmon and their winter supply of edible roots. In winter they hunted deer on snow shoes, and, as spring advanced, crossed the mountains to the headwaters of the Missouri to traffic in buffalo robes. You will see, therefore, that they were kept unusually busy, and red men have never shown a fondness for manual labor. But, beside this, they had numerous fights with enemies from the west, often losing some of their warriors and many of their horses.

At the time of the visit by our friends, Amokeat was principal chief of the Nez Perces. He and Mul-tal-la the Blackfoot were attached to each other, and the confidence of the latter in the dusky leader was complete. Had he not been so warm in his expressions of this faith in Amokeat, Deerfoot would never have left the stallion Whirlwind in his care while the explorers were pressing their way down the Columbia to tidewater.

As it was, the Shawanoe was troubled by misgivings from the hour he parted company with his matchless steed. As the distance between him and the Nez Perce village lessened, it was hard for the dusky youth to suppress his nervousness. He was reserved, speaking only now and then when necessary, and unconsciously hurrying his footsteps, until the brothers were ready to drop from exhaustion. Had the village been a mile farther off they would have been obliged to beg for rest.

The arrival of the party caused less excitement than would be supposed. The majority of the men and women were away, assisting in the harvesting of salmon, while fully a score of the ablest warriors were off somewhere in the mountains, either hunting or scouting, preparatory to some movement the Nez Perces as a tribe had in view. There were enough on hand, however, to give our friends due attention and to welcome them back.

The first inquiry of Deerfoot was as to the horses. To the south of the main village stretched an expanse of undergrowth, bushes, succulent grass and herbage, where the animals of the tribe were turned loose to roam at will when not needed by their owners. The Nez Perces, with gestures and the few words that were understood by Mul-tal-la, said the horses of their visitors would be found at the place described. It was not far off, and Deerfoot broke into a lope, his friends at his heels.

It required but a few minutes to reach the tract, which covered a number of acres. At different points glimpses were caught of horses cropping the grass and herbage. The first animal recognized was Zigzag, who was so near that the moment the party debouched into the space he raised his head, looked at them and gave a neigh of recognition. Then he resumed his grazing, as if he felt that he had done all the honors due from him.

"Yonder is Prince!" exclaimed Victor, running forward to greet his horse, while George Shelton began searching hither and yon for Jack. Mul-tal-la did not see Bug, and showed more interest in Deerfoot's search than in his own animal.

The Shawanoe had halted on the edge of the pasturage ground, glanced quickly over his field of vision, and then, placing a thumb and forefinger between his teeth, he emitted a blast like that of a steam whistle. It was a signal he had taught the stallion, and he knew that if the horse was within a mile he would come toward him on a full gallop. Deerfoot repeated the call twice and then waited and looked and listened. None of the horses so much as raised his head, and the heart of the youth became like lead.

"Whirlwind is not here," he said sadly to the Blackfoot. George and Victor hurried back, drawn by the signal whose meaning they understood. In truth, when they left his side it had been more for the purpose of hunting for the stallion than for their own animals. Their hearts ached for Deerfoot, whose face was the picture of disappointment and grief.

"Call to him again," suggested George.

"It can do no good. If he is near he would have heard Deerfoot; he is gone."

"He may have wandered beyond reach of your signal," said Victor. "You know he never felt friendly toward other horses and always kept by himself."

With a weak hope that his friend was right, Deerfoot walked a hundred yards to where an uprooted tree lay on its side, climbed upon the trunk, and, facing the different points of the compass in turn, whistled so shrilly that in the afternoon stillness the sound awoke the echoes for miles in every direction. Then he stood in the attitude of intense attention. Certain that the stallion had not gone far of his own accord, he knew these calls would bring him dashing to the spot, provided no person had had a hand in his disappearance.

But the minutes passed without anything of this nature occurring, and the Shawanoe sprang down from the slight elevation and came back to where his sympathizing friends awaited him. They were silent, for none could say aught to comfort him.

"We will look for Amokeat," he quietly remarked, leading the way to the village. There the inquiries of Mul-tal-la brought the first definite information of the missing horse. It was of anything but a pleasant nature.

It has been said that about a score of Nez Perce warriors were absent on a scouting or hunting expedition. They were under the lead of Amokeat, who rode away on the back of Whirlwind. They had been gone several days and were liable to return at any hour, or they might be absent for a week or more longer.

When Deerfoot gained this information he was filled with indignation. Without speaking, he turned his back upon his friends and walked to and fro for several minutes. He was striving to gain control of his emotions, and some time passed before he could do so. When he succeeded he rejoined his comrades, several of the Nez Perces gathering round and watching the four with no little curiosity.

"Amokeat did not ask Deerfoot that he might ride Whirlwind," said the Shawanoe, the flash not fully gone from his eyes, and a slight tremulousness showing in his voice.

"He had no business to do so," added the impulsive Victor; "I wonder that the horse allowed anyone to ride him except you."

George Shelton tried to soothe his troubled friend.

"I understand how you feel, Deerfoot, but it looks to me as if it will come out all right. The Nez Perces rode off on their horses, with Whirlwind in the lead. Why should they not come back the same way, with Whirlwind none the worse? Amokeat did not expect you for some time, and who can wonder that he wished to ride such a steed?"

Deerfoot turned and looked in the face of the lad.

"Does my brother wish Deerfoot to sit down and fold his hands and wait for days and weeks, all the time not knowing whether Whirlwind will come back again or not? Does not my brother see that there is not a day nor an hour to be wasted? Deerfoot would die many times while waiting for Amokeat; he cannot do it."

This was another way of declaring that the young Shawanoe meant to set out to recover his steed without an hour's unnecessary delay. All felt in the circumstances that it was the best thing to do. No one offered further suggestion. Mul-tal-la, who had spoken hardly a word, now told Deerfoot he would find out all that was to be learned of Amokeat and his party.

Left alone with the lads, the Shawanoe explained the plan he had formed.

"Mul-tal-la will take my brothers to his home among the Blackfeet, where they will stay until spring comes; winter is too near for them to travel any farther toward the Ohio. Mul-tal-la will make them welcome and they will not want for food and comforts."

"And what of *you*?"

"When Deerfoot meets Whirlwind, the two will join his brothers and all will be together till the sun begins to melt the snow on the sides of the mountains. Then they will set out for the Ohio which they left so many months ago."

"Will you make this search for Whirlwind on horseback or on foot?"

"On foot; there is no horse that can help me. Whirlwind would be offended if he saw me come after him on any other of these animals. Deerfoot can travel better on foot than any other way."

"You wish us to take our horses with us to the Blackfoot country?"

The Shawanoe nodded.

"Take the four and keep them among the Blackfeet; they will be needed by us when spring comes."

"You have plenty of bullets and powder. Is there anything of ours that you would like?" asked Victor.

"Yes,—*that*; it may be of help to Deerfoot."

The dusky youth pointed to the spyglass suspended by a cord around the neck of George Shelton. The owner instantly slipped the string over his head.

"You are welcome to it and to anything else of ours."

"Deerfoot thanks his brothers, but there is nothing more he wishes. He has his rifle, his powder horn, his bullet pouch, his flint and steel and his hunting knife. Anything more would be a burden, but his heart is warm with gratitude to his brothers."

At this point in the conversation, Mul-tal-la returned with news of what he had learned by his inquiries among the Nez Perces.

The knowledge amounted to little. Chief Amokeat had led his warriors northward three days before, starting just as the sun appeared. He gave no word as to when he would come back, and none could do anything more than guess, nor was the leader clear as to the nature of the business on which he ventured. Perhaps he himself did not know.

Still the task that Deerfoot had set himself seemed possible of accomplishment. Knowing the point at which the party left the village and the course taken by them, he could strike the trail, and to keep to it would not be more difficult than many feats he had performed amid the forests and canebrakes of Kentucky and Ohio. He made sure that there was no mistake at the beginning. Then he bade his friends good-bye.

Before doing so he talked for some minutes with Mul-tal-la. The Blackfoot favored the course Deerfoot had laid out for himself, though it was not unlikely that the fact that opposition was useless may have had its weight in the conclusion reached by Mul-tal-la. He told the Shawanoe that he would proceed straight to the Blackfoot country, and there await the coming of his friend, who expected like the boys to spend the winter in that northern region.

Deerfoot disliked "scenes" as much as did George and Victor Shelton. The only ceremony between him and the three was the shaking of hands and the expression of good wishes. Thus they parted. The dusky youth made his way directly to the point where he had been informed Amokeat and his party had left on their northward excursion, and, without looking behind him, found the trail and began his long journey.

Mul-tal-la waited for some minutes after his departure and then gave the word for the brothers to make ready. Accordingly, the horses were brought to the village, the saddles and bridles taken from the lodge of the chieftain, where they had been stored, together with the superfluous articles left behind when the explorers started on their canoe voyage down the Columbia. To this property was added that which had gone on the voyage. Everything was carefully packed on the back of Zigzag, saddles and bridles were put in place, all three mounted, waved good-bye and thanks to the Nez Perces, most of those that remained behind having gathered to see the visitors off. Then these in turn began the journey which was to take them through a pass in the Rocky Mountains and into the extensive Blackfoot country. For a time we will leave them to themselves and give our attention to Deerfoot, who was never more resolute of purpose than when he determined not to rejoin his friends until he had recovered Whirlwind, or at least gained tidings of him.

It may be said that the young Shawanoe was hopeful of finding the stallion unharmed, and he had reasonable ground for such hope. He could not help feeling displeased with the action of Amokeat, who certainly had presumed in thus using the property of another. Still, if no harm had befallen the steed, the Shawanoe would check the reproof he had in mind.

Several facts caused Deerfoot uneasiness. The beauty and nobleness of the stallion could not fail to excite envy wherever and by whomever seen. His owner believed that Amokeat would steal him if he had the chance, but it need not be explained that the circumstances rendered that impossible. In venturing upon this raid, the Nez Perces were sure to come in collision with hostile Indians. They had lost warriors and horses before. Indeed, their enemies had invaded the homes of the Nez Perces and robbed them. Suppose Amokeat and his companions got into a fight with some of the northern tribes. As likely as not the Nez Perces would be defeated. In that case, Whirlwind would be first of the spoils gathered in by the victors.

Suppose again the Nez Perces were victorious. The possession of the matchless stallion must be betrayed to their enemies, who would leave no stone unturned to capture him. There was every reason, too, to fear that the hostiles would be successful; for they would be in their own country and have every advantage on their side. With all the charity that Deerfoot could feel, he could not help condemning the Nez Perce chieftain for taking the great risk of causing the loss of Whirlwind.

You need hardly be reminded that if Deerfoot found this had taken place, he had no thought of giving up the hunt. If it was conceivable that the steed had fallen into the hands of the Eskimos, and they had journeyed to the Arctic circle with him, the Shawanoe would have kept straight on until he overtook the despoilers.

The Shawanoe gave a fine exhibition of his consummate skill in tracking a party of horsemen. When this party numbered a score, more or less, it was no trouble to keep to the trail, which was plainly marked; but had he done this his progress would have been delayed, for he would have had to follow every turning and doubling, which would have made the journey twice as lengthy as a straight line.

When Deerfoot was hardly a mile from the Nez Perce village he followed the footprints to the top of a ridge, where he paused and scanned the broad, mountainous country spread out before him. He knew the Nez Perces must have reached this point shortly after sunrise. He noted the general direction of the trail as it descended the slope in front, and accepted that as the course which the horsemen intended to follow. Then he fixed upon the point where they would be likely to make their midday halt. It was a clump of trees and undergrowth on the shores of a small lake, whose waters gleamed in the sun. Paying no further attention to the trail itself, Deerfoot set out at a swift lope for the body of water.

CHAPTER III.
THE TRAIL NORTHWARD.

The small lake which was the destination of Deerfoot seemed to be only two or three miles distant, but he knew it was all of twenty miles away. Being on foot, he took the most direct course. The route of the horses was of necessity so tortuous and difficult that it must have been fully a half greater than the direct one. The task was so easy for the Shawanoe that he did not lope or run, but kept up his swinging gait, which caused him not the least fatigue. Now and then he was forced to make a circuit around a mass of rocks, or a densely wooded section, but these diversions were of little account. They might have been twice as extensive and still he would not have minded them.

When near the body of water he climbed another ridge, upon whose crest the growth of wood was slight, and took a sweeping survey of the surrounding country. The scenery was magnificent and impressive. Far to the northward rose a towering range of mountains, whose snowy peaks pierced the sky and suggested enormous white clouds piled against the horizon. To the west rose another range, one of whose summits was loftier than any within his range of vision. Seen in the far distance, the soft air gave it a slight bluish tint, which gradually dissolved into fleecy whiteness toward the crest. To the eastward the landscape was made up of ridges, elevations and valleys, with growths of pine, cedar, oak and other species of wood. The lake's outlet was toward the west, winding in and out among the depressions until a curve hid it from sight fully a score of miles away.

There was a biting sharpness in the air that told of the nearness of winter, for the month of November was come, and in that northern latitude the rigorous season would soon set in. A whiff of air which fanned the face of the Indian brought the chill of snow and ice in it, while here and there the leaves of some of the deciduous trees drifted downward like the soft falling flakes of snow.

Deerfoot raised the glass to his eyes and slowly swept the field of vision. It was a striking proof of the solitude of this immense region that he did not see the first sign of a human being. No horsemen riding across the open spaces or climbing the wooded heights formed a part of the picture, nor in any direction could he detect the faint smoke of a camp fire. Wherever the Nez Perces whom he was pursuing might be, they were still a long distance away.

But the diversified landscape did not lack animal life. The most interesting sight was that of two grizzly bears, that were frolicking like a couple of puppies in an open space at the foot of a slight elevation. Deerfoot held the glass pointed at them for some minutes and more than once smiled at the odd picture. The great hulking brutes tumbled, rolled, pawed and boxed each other, all the while pretending to bite and yet taking care that neither tooth nor nail did harm. Then one would start to run off, as if frightened, with the other in hot pursuit. When overtaken, and sometimes before, the fugitive would wheel and cuff and bite at the other, as if in a dreadful rage. You know how amusing the antics of kittens and puppies are. Imagine, if you can, two enormous bears disporting themselves in the same comical fashion, and you will understand why the Shawanoe watched the couple minute after minute, forgetting for the time the serious business on which he was engaged.

But this was not all that attracted him in his surroundings. From out the undergrowth on the northern side of the stream forming the outlet of the lake came two or three hundred buffaloes, their dusky bodies imparting a strange appearance of agitation to that portion of the landscape. They headed for the stream, which was no more than a hundred feet in width, and plunged in, pausing long enough to drink, flirting their tails and tossing their heads, bellowing and crowding one another. The water was too shallow to force them to swim, but it was splashed and flung in all directions. When those at the front emerged they broke into a gallop, with the others dashing tumultuously after them.

Their course brought them within a few rods of the base of the elevation on which Deerfoot was standing. He walked down the slope until quite near the head of the herd, when he brought his rifle to his shoulder and sent a bullet just back of the foreleg of one of the bulls. The stricken beast made a single plunging dive and then rolled over dead. Being on the fringe of the herd he was not trampled upon, and none of his companions paid any attention to him. The bison is—or rather *was*—a stupid creature, his own destruction often resulting from his lack of ordinary intelligence.

Deerfoot waited until the last animal had passed, when he went forward to where the carcass of the game lay and deftly extracted its tongue. He did not touch any other portion, but, washing the delicacy in the stream, carried it to the small grove of trees which he had fixed upon in his mind as the place of the encampment of the Nez Perces, on their first day after leaving their village.

Before he reached the shelter of the clump of trees the quick eye of the Shawanoe saw the imprints of hoofs, and signs of a party of horsemen having halted at the spot. Chief Amokeat and his Nez Perces had made their first meal on fish drawn from the lake, as was shown by the fragments of their feast scattered round. Considerable ashes indicated the spot where a fire had been kindled, in the usual primitive manner of spinning a light pointed stick, whose sharpened end was thrust into another dry branch.

Thus Deerfoot's calculations proved to be right. He had reached the scene of the midday halt of the Nez Perces by traveling about two-thirds of the distance of his predecessors. With his flint and steel he soon had a blaze going. Over it he broiled the bison tongue, cut into thin strips, and ate his fill. The meal was a big one for him, and he would not go out of his way to procure any more food for twenty-four hours or more. Taking a long draught from the cold, crystalline waters, he resumed his journey, which was due north, his blanket fastened about his shoulders, and his rifle sometimes resting in the crook made by bending his left arm at the elbow, after the style of modern sportsmen, held sometimes in a trailing position, and again reposing upon his shoulder.

For two miles or more he kept to the trail, inasmuch as it was direct and nothing was to be gained by leaving it. With his senses alert, he finally turned to the right, in order to take advantage of a mass of rocks on ground so elevated that a more extensive view than the former one could be secured. He climbed as nimbly as a monkey to the top, glanced over the many square miles spread out before his gaze and then looked northward.

Ah! he saw something suggestive. The glass was pointed toward the spot and instantly confirmed the unaided eye. In the horizon, in the mist of a stretch of wooded country, he observed a faint, almost invisible line of vapor climbing upward into the cold blue sky, and gradually dissolving, until at the height of a hundred feet or less all trace of it vanished.

The most careful scrutiny could not tell anything more. The spot was between fifteen and twenty miles away, with the roughest sort of country intervening. It was a good day's journey distant, but in the same moment that Deerfoot made his interesting discovery he resolved to thread his way to the place without a minute's halt on his part until he reached his destination.

His quick mind instantly saw several explanations of the "sign." It could not be the Nez Perces riding north, for it was impossible that they had lagged to such an extent on the road. If it was Amokeat and his party, they must be returning from their raid, or hunting expedition, or whatever had engaged their energies. It would seem more likely that the Indians belonged to some other tribe. Be that as it may, the only means of answering the question was by finding out for himself, and that Deerfoot started to do with the grim, unshakable resolution of his nature.

With all his matchless swiftness and endurance, he would not have been able to travel the distance until the night was well advanced; for, though there were numerous places where he broke into his fleet lope, and more than once rose to a higher pace, he was compelled to make detours that greatly lengthened the distance and added to the labor. Again, a moderate walk was the best he could do.

About the middle of the afternoon he came upon the bank of a deep, swift stream fully a hundred yards wide. No doubt he could have found a ford had he taken the time to search for it, but the minutes were too valuable to waste. With hardly a moment's hesitation he took three steps over the flinty floor, and then found he had to swim. He had not so much as loosened the blanket looped about his shoulders and which threatened to interfere with the movements of his arms. He held his rifle above his head, so as to prevent any water running into the barrel, either at the muzzle or by percolation at the vent, and swam with his other arm and his feet. For a portion of the way he "trod water," apparently with the same ease that he walked upon solid earth. So he overcame the powerful current and emerged almost directly opposite the point where he had entered. You will remember that in approaching the stream he left the trail some time before, but he knew it was not far off, and doubtless would have led him to a ford. That he would not dally long enough to hunt out the more convenient crossing place was another illustration of Deerfoot's indifference to his own comfort. What though his garments were dripping when he stepped upon solid earth again, and the air was almost wintry in its chill, he cared naught. The exercise threw his frame into a glow and the moisture gradually left his clothing.

A few miles farther and the Shawanoe solved one question over which he had been speculating. In the distance he caught sight of a party of horsemen approaching from the direction of the camp whose smoke he had noticed hours before. They were no more than two or three miles distant, and when first seen were coming almost in a direct line for Deerfoot.

The first sight was that of a single horseman, who had ridden up the farther side of a slope, and came into view as he neared the top. Without pausing, he began the descent, and was followed by others, all in single file, until seventeen rode into the field of vision. Before Deerfoot brought his glass into use he had recognized the horsemen as Nez Perces. They were returning from their expedition, and if the statement of the number that had left home was correct, had lost at least three.

The spyglass disclosed the chieftain Amokeat to the Shawanoe, who, with his horse on a walk, was riding at the head of the procession. The instrument revealed another significant fact:

Neither Amokeat nor any of his warriors was mounted on Whirlwind.

Deerfoot had to struggle to restrain his indignation. Had he been within reach of Amokeat at that moment, it is not unlikely he would have dragged him from his horse and given him a lesson he could never forget. The very thing the Shawanoe had feared from the first had occurred: the stallion was either stolen or dead.

But as Deerfoot advanced to meet the party, who soon observed and identified him, he pulled himself together. It would have taken one who knew him intimately, like Simon Kenton, or George or Victor Shelton, to read in the slightly pale face and peculiar gleam of the dark eyes the evidence of the emotion that the Shawanoe held well under control.

It was in the depth of a broad valley, where there was a semblance to a trail which had been made by bison or other animals on their way to water, that Chief Amokeat drew up and awaited the approach of the Shawanoe. The latter, as was his custom, made a half-military salute, and, without any more preliminaries came to the point. He used the Blackfoot tongue, which was familiar to the Nez Perce.

"Deerfoot seeks his horse. Where is he?"

Amokeat must have expected the question, for he shook his head and answered in the language of the Blackfeet:

"Amokeat is grieved to tell Deerfoot he will never see the horse he loves again. It saddens the heart of Amokeat, but he speaks with a single tongue."

"Is my horse dead?"

"That Amokeat does not know. Yesterday the Assiniboines took him from us, and they are now far on their way to their villages."

"Why did Amokeat take my horse from where Deerfoot had left him? Why did he not wait until he could see Deerfoot and ask him. He has stolen my horse."

This was a pointed charge, but Deerfoot could not wholly curb his anger. The chief, however, did not seem to feel the sting of the words, though more than one of his warriors, who had drawn up their horses and were looking on and listening, showed resentment.

Amokeat now proceeded to tell in his own way what had befallen him and his companions. He said they had started out for a hunt, though expecting to have an encounter with some of their enemies before their return. At a point about a hundred miles to the northeast, while riding through a cañon, they were suddenly attacked by fully a hundred red men, whom they recognized as Assiniboines that were a long way from their hunting grounds.

While it is more than likely the Nez Perce leader exaggerated the number of his assailants, no doubt they were superior to the smaller company. The latter put up a brave fight, but before they could extricate themselves from the trap five of their number were shot from their horses. This statement showed that originally the Nez Perces numbered more than a score.

Amokeat was on the back of Whirlwind, who carried him off with such amazing speed that he was soon separated from his warriors. Deerfoot's lips curled when he heard this statement, for to him it was a proof of the cowardice of the chief. The party had no time to recover the bodies of their fallen comrades, who were left to be scalped and despoiled by the victors, the stray horses also passing into the hands of the Assiniboines.

Amokeat was in full flight when, in dashing through a mass of undergrowth, he suddenly came face to face with eight or ten Assiniboines (probably the number was less). He was ambushed so cleverly that escape was out of the question. He would have resisted, however, had not one of his enemies called out that he wished to have a parley with him.

This warrior, who was the leader of the little party, told Amokeat that if he would swap the black stallion he rode for the pony of the Assiniboines, the chief would not be harmed, but would be left free to go to his own home. Had the grinning Nez Perce put his conclusion in English, it would have been something like this:

"I counted myself most fortunate, for what was to prevent the Assiniboines from shooting me from the back of the stallion and then taking him away with them? So the trade was made and he is now in the hands of the Assiniboines."

CHAPTER IV.
THE LAND OF THE ASSINIBOINES.

As Deerfoot listened to the story of the Nez Perce leader his gorge steadily rose, for the account was worse, if possible, than he had expected to hear. Not only did he resent the cool appropriation of his steed by Amokeat, but he read the proof of the cowardice of the chief, who had deserted his companions when in peril and then, instead of making a brave defence when cornered by the Assiniboines, had eagerly passed over to them the property of another in order to secure his own safety.

The Shawanoe could not trust himself any further in the presence of Amokeat, who sat on the back of his pony and looked serenely down in his face, exulting over his own escape from the revenge of an enemy.

"Amokeat is a dog!" exclaimed Deerfoot, compressing his lips, turning around and walking from the presence of the chief and his party. He was on the alert, for he half expected an attack from more than one of them. If they had such action in mind, it was changed by the command of the leader, who called to them to follow him as he resumed the journey toward his own village.

The Shawanoe had learned several important facts. Whirlwind had passed from the hands of the Nez Perces to those of a wandering band of Assiniboines, whose villages and hunting grounds lay well to the northeast, some below and some above the boundary line in the country of the Saskatchewan. Thither the Shawanoe would go, though knowing absolutely nothing of the region or the people. In his contemptuous scorn of Amokeat, Deerfoot did not so much as look behind him until the afternoon was nearly gone and night was closing in. Then, when he turned his gaze to the rear, he saw nothing of men or horses.

He was thinking hard. It was evident that the only course which promised hope was for him to keep to the trail left by the Nez Perces until he reached the scene of the fight. From that point he would be guided by the footprints of the Assiniboine animals. Of course there was no distinguishable difference between those of Whirlwind and the impressions made by any other of his species, but there ought to be little difficulty in keeping to the main trail until he ran the party down.

You will understand that a number of puzzling complications threatened. It might be that the Assiniboines would continue their hunting or raiding excursions for days, turning off and pushing to the south or east or west, with a view of attacking some of the tribes within United States territory. The Shawanoe hoped that such would be the course of the raiders, for it would simplify the situation. He would have a small party to operate against, instead of a whole village or tribe.

A singular difficulty presented itself. Deerfoot relied upon entering the Assiniboine settlements or joining the raiders without rousing any suspicion of his real errand. Then he would content himself in patience and await a chance of slipping off with Whirlwind. The likelihood of gaining such opportunity would be almost destroyed if his errand became known. Now, the danger of betrayal was in the stallion himself. He could not be made to understand the need of cunning and silence, but was sure to show his joy at sight of his owner. When this was observed by his captors, they would be certain to connect it with the long journey of the stranger, who would then have all he could do to guard his own life.

Reflecting over this probable phase of the situation, Deerfoot decided what his own conduct should be. He resolved that if Whirlwind made a rush for him, thereby revealing the truth, he would leap upon his back, throw himself forward, and send the steed flying off at the highest speed. There would be imminent risk of both being shot before they could pass beyond range, but the danger would be no greater than the Shawanoe had faced many times, and still he did not bear a scar upon his body.

His plan, however, was to rely upon subtlety. If he could succeed in locating his pet, he would keep out of the animal's sight until the crisis came. He knew Whirlwind was alive, and was not very far off. Less than two days previous he had passed over the same spot, and the trail left by him and his companions could be readily followed.

So it was that the young Shawanoe pressed forward with long, swift strides until the gloom shut out all sight of the footprints. He could calculate quite closely from the different landmarks the course followed by the Nez Perces, but he determined to run no chances. Time was too precious, and he was resolved not to go astray.

He was in a wild, mountainous country, interspersed with ridges, isolated peaks and lofty ranges. There were numerous valleys, cañons, gorges and ravines, with stretches of wood and stunted undergrowth. The sound of falling waters, cascades and rapids was hardly ever absent. Naturally the horsemen had sought the most favorable route, keeping mainly to the valleys, but occasionally riding over elevated portions. Thus the course was easier for Deerfoot than it would have been had the party been on foot like himself. The Assiniboines were not likely to make haste, for they had no reason for doing so. With his long strides, his lope and occasional running, as the ground offered the chance, the pursuer knew he was gaining upon those whom he was so anxious to overtake.

When night had fairly come, Deerfoot sought out a place among the rocks in which to sleep. He did not look for food, nor did he so much as drink from the mountain stream that he heard rippling near at hand. It took some time to find a suitable spot for a bed. He fixed upon a cavity large enough for him to stretch out with his blanket wrapped about him. He could have readily kindled a fire, but preferred not to do so, since it was liable to draw the attention of wild animals, or possibly of those of his own race who might be in the vicinity. As it was, a prowling wolf or bear might threaten, but the youth felt no misgiving when, after spending a brief time in prayer, he lay down and speedily sank into slumber.

At the first streakings of light he was on his feet. Praying again, he fastened his blanket about his shoulders, knelt at the mountain stream, drank deeply, bathed face and hands and was off once more. No move was made toward procuring the morning meal, which most folks in his situation would have found indispensable.

The trail was clearly marked, but before resuming his pursuit Deerfoot climbed to the highest elevation near at hand and spent a few minutes in studying the surrounding country. The main features were similar to those already described, except perhaps in the increase of the ruggedness of the scenery. He was within the Rocky Mountain district, but kept mainly to the foothills, where journeying was easier than among the mountains themselves.

Noting that the general course of the trail he was following up was from the northeast, he scanned with special interest the country in that direction. He picked out a point some twenty miles distant as the place where the Nez Perces were most likely to have made one of their camps. While he might have shortened the time by keeping a direct line to it, he stuck to his resolution not to turn aside from the trail.

Though he did not catch sight of any horseman, he saw that which roused his curiosity. Hardly a mile away he observed a single Indian coming toward him on foot. It may be said the stranger leaped into view, for Deerfoot was looking over a certain spot at the country beyond when a peculiar, flitting movement caused him to depress his glass to learn the cause.

The Indian seemed to have been following a roughly marked path, when he came to a huge boulder, which, instead of passing around, he climbed, walked across the top, and then dropped to the ground again. It was this action which caused Deerfoot to turn his gaze upon him.

Under the glass the stranger was seen with as much distinctness as if he were only a few rods distant. When looking at him the Shawanoe, for the first time in his life, saw a dwarf belonging to his own race. The man had broad shoulders and body and sturdy legs, but his height could not have been more than four and a half feet. Moreover he was very bow-legged, was a hunchback, had a broad mouth, a flat nose and small twinkling eyes. His long black hair dangled loosely about his shoulders, he was clad in a hunting dress similar to that worn by the Shawanoe, except that he was without a blanket, and his clothing was much shabbier. He carried a bow fully double his own length, and advanced with a curious sidelong, wabbling gait, which accented more strikingly his difference from those of his own people.

When the astonished Deerfoot had noted these peculiarities, he scanned the vicinity of the dwarf for his companions. None was seen, and our friend decided that the fellow was entirely alone. It was impossible to make a guess as to the tribe to which he belonged, though Deerfoot suspected, without any particular reason, that he was an Assiniboine. As to how he came to be by himself, and traveling southward, no theory could be formed by the astute Shawanoe.

The latter lowered his glass, and, standing in full view, watched the hunchback as he drew near with his crab-like, wabbling gait. Although the Shawanoe was a much more conspicuous object on the landscape, it was evident the other did not discover him until he was almost within a hundred yards. No better proof could have been asked that the stranger was afflicted with poor eyesight.

Suddenly he descried the form on the rocks and stopped short. He was startled. Then he began hurriedly drawing an arrow from the bundle hung behind his shoulder. It was a curious coincidence, which caught Deerfoot's notice, that the dwarf was left-handed like himself. The latter laid his gun at his feet and raised both hands above his head, a sign of friendship. The stranger paused in his warlike preparations, but seemed in doubt whether to launch a missile or to accept the sign of comity. Deerfoot picked up his weapon, held his other hand over his head, and began carefully descending the elevation. He kept a close watch on the other, for he half expected he would let fly with his arrow, and it would have been unpleasant, to say the least, to act as a target, even at a considerable distance. The dwarf stood motionless, closely watching the Shawanoe as he came toward him, evidently doubting and hesitating, but Deerfoot kept up his signs of goodwill, which the other could not fail to understand.

It is not unreasonable to believe that the personality of Deerfoot had much to do with removing the misgivings of the stranger, for the smiling face of the Shawanoe as he drew near would have impressed anyone, though Deerfoot himself would never have admitted anything of the kind. Be that as it may, the meeting was friendly, though Deerfoot did not offer his hand in greeting, for he thought it unlikely that the other would have understood the meaning of the salutation.

He addressed the stranger in the Blackfoot tongue, only to receive a shake of the head in reply. The dwarf did not understand a syllable. In response, he used a language that was "all Greek" to the Shawanoe. There was no common ground, except that of signs, upon which the two could meet, and that was of slight service.

"Assiniboine? Assiniboine?" asked Deerfoot, with a marked rising inflection. Another shake of the head might indicate a denial of such tribal relation, or what was more likely, a failure to comprehend the question. Deerfoot repeated the word "Nez Perce," and was replied to as before.

The first bit of information that the Shawanoe could gather for a time was that the Indian of abbreviated stature came from the north. That was clearly established, as was the direction which he was following, but nothing was brought to light as to the nature of his errand in the south.

The thought had been in the mind of our friend from the first that this misshapen red man had seen the party of Assiniboines who held Whirlwind. How was the question to be asked?

Deerfoot stepped to a tree resembling the water maple that grew a few feet to the right of them. Its diameter was a foot or more. With his hunting knife he cut out a square some six inches in diameter and carefully peeled it off, the other attentively watching him all the time.

Deerfoot now proceeded to trace on the filmy inner side of the bark with the point of his knife the outlines of a horse with unusually long tail and mane. This done, he depicted a warrior sitting on him with no saddle except a blanket and without bridle. When the crude but symmetrical picture was finished, he handed the piece of bark to the other. The dwarf studied it a minute or two with close interest, Deerfoot meanwhile watching his countenance.

Suddenly the homely visage lit up. The stranger recognized the figure of the beautiful stallion. He had seen him!

With a thrill of hope the Shawanoe pointed north, his gesture clearly meaning that he wished to know whether it was there the animal had been met. The stranger shook his head. Deerfoot was disappointed, fearing his meaning had not been understood. It seemed to him that the Assiniboine horsemen must be journeying in that direction, and the negative motion of the other's head might indicate that he did not catch the drift of the question.

Deerfoot now pointed toward the rising sun, only to be answered by another shake of his head. He next indicated the northeast. The dwarf nodded vigorously several times. Then he gazed steadily into the handsome face and began circling one of his hands rapidly around his head, pointing to his moccasins and then to the sky. These peculiar gestures were repeated a number of times, when they ceased as abruptly as they began.

The Shawanoe could not form the first idea of what the man was trying to say, nor did he ever learn.

The dwarf perceived that he could not make himself understood, gave up the effort, and with an awkward good-bye resumed his tramp southward. Uncertain of what whim might suddenly take possession of him, Deerfoot, while also moving in the opposite direction, kept a furtive watch to the rear. He did not see the dwarf look behind him and it is not probable that he meditated any wrong.

The Shawanoe was not satisfied with what had occurred. Glancing down at the trail and as far ahead as it could be traced, he saw that its course was due north. He believed that it led for a long way toward that point of the compass. If such proved the fact the hunchback had tried to deceive the inquirer by making him believe that Whirlwind was to be sought to the northeast. The Shawanoe could no longer doubt that the nature of his inquiry had been understood, and the reply of the dwarf was clear. Deerfoot was inclined to believe the strange creature really belonged to the Assiniboine tribe and was trying to shield his countrymen.

Moreover, the Shawanoe knew little of this people. He understood in a vague way that their homes were well to the northward, and partly in another country than the United States. The true direction, however, was to the northeast. Thus the Indian of abbreviated stature had indicated the right course after all.

Adhering to his policy, Deerfoot wasted no time. While these thoughts were passing through his mind, he was loping forward with the trail still as his guide, and had not gone two miles when he came upon the scene of the fight between the Assiniboines and the Nez Perces.

CHAPTER V.
A WELCOME SIGHT.

The first sign that caught the eye of the Shawanoe was the mute forms of the five Nez Perces, stretched here and there over a space of an eighth of a mile. All had been scalped and mutilated. But he had seen such shocking sights before, and he did not go near the bodies nor give them further attention. It was no great task for him to transfer his interest from the trail of one party to that of another, and he was speedily loping forward as rapidly as before.

To his astonishment he had gone only a little way when he discovered a marked change of course. The Assiniboine footprints pointed to the northeast. The information gained from the dwarf was reliable; the horsemen were heading for their own villages.

The Shawanoe called all his consummate woodcraft into play to determine how much time had passed since the party rode over this ground. He figured that it must have been on the previous day, though such conclusion did not fully accord with what was told him by the chieftain Amokeat. His opinion of that leader, however, made him ready to believe anything ill of him.

If the horsemen had twenty-four hours the start of their pursuer, and kept up their rapid flight, he could hardly expect to come up with them for several days. Deerfoot believed he could steadily gain, but he was on foot and they were mounted. Such gain, in the most favorable circumstances, must be gradual. Had they halted for any length of time, or diverged from the regular course, the prospect would be all the more favorable for him.

With this theory, Deerfoot now made a change of policy. Instead of keeping to the trail with all its windings (made in order to accommodate the horses), he adopted his other recourse—that of reasoning out the route most likely to be followed by the warriors, and, fixing upon a camp far in advance, making his way thither by the most direct course. Provided he fell into no error, he would thus save miles of distance and hours of time.

It was still early in the day when he forded a narrow, rapid stream, in which the water rose to his waist, and climbing the nearest elevation, which was a ridge crowned with rocks and a few stunted cedars, he paused to make a study of the country spread before him.

Naturally his first scrutiny was directed to the northeast. In that direction the surface was rolling, with numerous valleys and mountain spurs, but none of the latter was of great height. The towering peaks rose more to the north and west. There was variety and yet sameness in the vast undulating expanse, with its wealth of wood, of rocks, some bleak and dark of color, and others fringed with vegetation, of swelling hills, many of which elsewhere would have been called mountains, and beautiful valleys, with numerous streams hidden through most of their flow, all seeking an outlet in the Atlantic or Pacific, hundreds of miles away.

The bed of one mountain torrent could be traced for a long distance by the mist that hovered over it, though the spectator could not catch the first sight of the water itself. At another point to the right the Shawanoe saw what appeared to be a curved streak of silver, fifty feet in height and but two or three feet wide. It looked to be absolutely motionless, and yet it was a waterfall, from whose foamy base little clouds of steam floated upward or were wafted aside by the wisps of wind.

Deerfoot refrained from using the instrument until he had done all he could with his unaided vision. His reason for this was his wish to place himself in the same situation as the Assiniboine party. None of them knew what a spyglass is, and he tried to reason from what he saw upon what point they would be likely to fix as their halting place.

Had he known the precise minute or hour when the horsemen had ridden past the spot near where he was standing, the problem would have been easy of solution, but no Indian or white hunter ever lived who could settle such a question without more definite data. We hear stories of achievements of that nature, but most of them are mythical, though the woodcraft of many a trailer has enabled him to do things which to others were impossible.

The Shawanoe believed the Assiniboines had ridden past at a moderate pace about the middle of the preceding day. Acting on that supposition, he selected a point somewhat more than a dozen miles to the northeast as the one where they would have been likely to encamp for the night. The trouble was that there was little in the wooded place, near a small body of water, bearing a striking resemblance to the lake of the previous day, to favor it above others in the neighborhood. They might have halted several miles beyond or that much nearer the standpoint of the Shawanoe.

At the best it was guesswork; but having made his conjecture, Deerfoot now raised the glass to his eyes and centered his attention upon the spot. As he did so he was thrilled by a discovery which set his nerves at once on edge.

On the edge of the trees, near the lake itself, he saw two Indians, standing as if in conversation. When he lowered the glass it was impossible to make them out at so great distance, but the instrument revealed them clearly. Suddenly one of the couple came forward to the body of water, lay down on his face and drank. The other walked part of the way and then stopped, and was rejoined by the former. It looked as if they resumed their converse over some subject in which they were unusually interested.

Deerfoot was almost certain that the two were members of the party for whom he was hunting. If such were the fact, something must have occurred to cause them to linger on their return to their villages.

While he was speculating as to whether this was probable, smoke began filtering through the tops of the pines, behind the couple. A fire had been started, though the hour of day was one when the party naturally would have been in motion.

The question remained as to whether the horsemen intended to stay where they were until the morrow or would soon resume their journey. The last supposition seemed the most likely.

The decision of the Shawanoe was to lessen the distance between him and the horsemen while such a fine opportunity offered. Flinging the glass over his shoulder he set out to overtake the party in advance, doing his best to decide upon the right policy, now that the important information had come to him.

The most puzzling phase of the situation has been explained. But for the certain recognition that Whirlwind would make of his master, the latter would have gone direct to the Assiniboine camp and watched for his opportunity; but as nearly as he could determine there must be fully a score if not more of the warriors. To "cut out" the stallion from among them when the sun was shining was clearly an impossibility, though, as has been intimated, Deerfoot was ready to make the attempt if no other chance offered.

Discretion warned him to keep out of sight of the party until nightfall. He could then reconnoiter the camp with good prospect of getting Whirlwind away. If the Assiniboines placed a sentinel on duty, Deerfoot was confident he could get the better of him in the darkness. The raiders would not be looking for any attack, though when on the war trail they were sure to adopt the usual precautions.

The Shawanoe, therefore, had not gone far when he decided upon his plan of action. He would stay out of sight of men and animals until the gloom gave him his opportunity. Meanwhile it was well to decrease the intervening distance so far as was prudent.

It was yet early in the afternoon when the interval was cut in half. While doing this he stopped and made frequent surveys of the lake and wood. It would have made no great difference had he been observed by the horsemen, for it was impossible for them to suspect his identity or his business. Still, it was just as well to have his presence in the neighborhood unknown and unsuspected.

All this time the vapor was climbing through the tree tops. Those who had kindled the fire were still there, for they could not leave by the "back door" without being seen by the vigilant Shawanoe. He was surprised that none showed himself during these hours. The couple who had first caught his eye had disappeared long before in the wood and remained out of sight.

His interest led Deerfoot to continue edging forward until, by the close of the afternoon, he was within a mile of the camp. He had accomplished this by taking advantage of all the protection possible. Since plenty offered, and the Assiniboines were not apprehending anything of that nature, the task was not so hard as it might seem.

The weather remained clear, though still keen and cold. The Shawanoe had not eaten food for a long time, but he gave no thought to that. He was ready to wait until the morrow before satisfying his hunger. His one resolution was to regain Whirlwind, if such a feat was within the range of human possibility.

The young Shawanoe did not forget that he was acting upon a theory that might prove a rope of sand. The camp which he was reconnoitering with such care might be that of another party, even though they were Assiniboines. The probabilities, however, justified him in believing he was on the right track.

A curious feature of the situation was that he had not as yet seen a single horse. When a company of Indians stopped to rest, even for a short time, they were accustomed to allow their animals to graze. Between the margin of wood and the lake the dull green of grass was plainly perceptible. Perhaps there was some open spot among the trees which offered better pasturage for the horses. Deerfoot could not feel clear in his own mind as to the explanation of the absence of all sight of the animals.

He was speculating as to the cause of this singular fact when six horses issued from among the timber and came frolicking and cavorting down to the water's margin, where they thrust their noses into the lake to drink. No Indians showed themselves, the training of the animals making it unnecessary to guard them.

One of the steeds emerged from a point several yards to the right of the others and kept apart from them, as if he felt too proud to associate with those of common blood. When he lowered his head he was fully a couple of rods from his companions. This horse was the stallion Whirlwind.

"This Horse was Whirlwind."

The sight of his peerless creature threw the Shawanoe into a flutter, and it required all his self-control to restrain himself from running forward and calling to Whirlwind to meet him, but he resolutely held his ground, sheltered behind the projection of the boulder he had used as a screen in keeping the camp under surveillance. The situation was so critical that Deerfoot perhaps was over-cautious.

He reasoned keenly. A mile separated steed and master. The latter could have no thought that the youth from whom he had been separated for weeks was near. If Deerfoot emitted his piercing whistle the call would not be recognized on the instant, and the animal would be confused. The dress of Deerfoot and his appearance were so similar to those of other Indians that Whirlwind would not be likely to identify him until they came considerably nearer each other. The Assiniboines were in camp. They, too, would hear the signal and be quick to discover what it meant. Rather than have the black stallion escape from their possession they would shoot him as he ran. A red man always prefers to slay a captive rather than surrender him. With the horse shot Deerfoot would be forced to have it out with the warriors at such disadvantage that only one result could follow, for the Assiniboines were not only armed with guns—at least several were thus equipped—but they were daring and resolute.

It was these fears which caused the young Shawanoe to decide to remain in hiding until nightfall, which was now at hand. It is quite probable that the plan of calling Whirlwind to him would have succeeded, as the youth afterward admitted; but it certainly would have been attended with risk of failure, and he never regretted the decision he made within the same minute that he caught sight of his equine friend.

Like the king that he was, the stallion, having drank his fill, wheeled and with dignified step passed back among the trees, keeping apart from the others, who would have felt (as had Zigzag felt) the impact of the fiercely driven heels had they ventured upon any familiarity.

So it came about that Deerfoot the Shawanoe stayed in concealment until the gathering gloom shut out the grove and its occupants. There was no moon, but the star-gleam was strong and gave him all the light he wished. He preferred that to stronger illumination.

During the slow passing minutes that the youth waited he reached the conclusion that the Assiniboines in the timber were only a part of the horsemen that had overthrown the Nez Perces. Some cause had led them to divide, and a half dozen or so were waiting for the others to rejoin them. Why this separation had taken place Deerfoot could not understand, nor did he allow himself to be interested in the question. The reason for his belief lay in the number of horses that had issued from among the trees. In the circumstances, all the animals would have gone for water at the same time.

Deerfoot was cool, calm and perfectly poised when he stepped from behind the boulder and began his stealthy approach to the Assiniboine camp. He loosed his blanket from the fastening which held the fold together in front and laid it over his right arm. He confidently expected a fight and did not mean to have his limbs hampered. Instinctively he slipped his hand down to his girdle. The knife was there. He had examined his rifle long before. The charge and priming were as they should be, and he grasped the weapon with his left hand. He gave no thought to the fact that more than twenty-four hours had passed since he had eaten food. He was accustomed to such abstinence and the situation drove away all appetite. He would not have taken a dozen paces to the right or left to pick up nourishment.

A complication was threatened by the return of the other Assiniboines, but aside from that Deerfoot did not mean to wait a half hour longer than was necessary. His stealthy approach was continued until in the gloom he made out the dim outlines of the timber. The western terminus of the lake lay just to the left, so that in order to reach the camp he had to diverge for some rods in that direction. But the way was clear and the brief circuit brought him to the edge of the wood, with the calm sheet of water stretching for a half mile to the east, which was on his right hand.

The first step was to locate the Indians and their horses, for the wise general acquaints himself with the battle ground upon which the momentous issue is to be decided. The twinkle of light that glimmered among the trees guided the Shawanoe, and with little trouble he gained a position from which, unsuspected by the Assiniboines, he had a perfect view of them.

CHAPTER VI.
COMRADES TRUE.

The picture upon which Deerfoot looked recalled many similar ones in Ohio and Kentucky. There were six warriors seated on the ground, most of the party in lolling postures, three smoking long-stemmed pipes, and all had evidently partaken of food a short time before, for a faint odor of broiling venison or bison meat was in the air, and the signs within the camp showed that a meal had been prepared and eaten.

The burning sticks were piled against the base of a tree more than two feet in diameter and were burning so vigorously that the circle of light reached well beyond the group and pierced the shadows among the pines and cedars. A brief survey of the group left no doubt that they were awaiting the arrival of friends, as they had been doing for hours past, and might continue to do through the remaining night.

There was no reason why the Shawanoe should lose any time in surveying the Assiniboines, for he felt no interest in them. He was surprised to note that every one had a rifle, none being armed with the primitive bow and arrows. He tarried only long enough to decide in his mind who was the leader, and therefore the new proprietor of Whirlwind. Deerfoot had no special enmity against him, for it was Amokeat, the Nez Perce chieftain, who was responsible for the loss of the stallion.

The Shawanoe had straightened up and was silently withdrawing from his advanced position, holding the sheltering tree between him and the camp fire, when he was startled by a whinny from some point in the gloom close at hand. Turning his head he caught the dim outlines of Whirlwind making his way among the trees toward him. The sagacious stallion, through that wonderfully acute sense of smell which his species often show, had discovered the proximity of his master and had set out to find him. The space between the two was so brief that Deerfoot had hardly paused and looked behind him when the silken nose of Whirlwind was thrust against his face, and after his old fashion he touched his tongue to the cool cheek of his master and then affectionately rested his head on his shoulder.

It was a critical situation, for the steed had already warned the Assiniboines that something unusual was going on, but the delight and gratitude of the Shawanoe were so deep that he could not deny himself the pleasure of caressing his steed. He touched his lips to his nose, patted his forehead and neck and murmured:

"Whirlwind! Deerfoot's heart is thankful! He is happy, for he has found his best friend. No one shall part us again!"

But in that joyful moment the delicate situation could not be forgotten. Instead of leaping upon the back of the horse where the trees and limbs would interfere with a rapid flight, in addition to placing the rider at a disadvantage in case of attack, Deerfoot told Whirlwind to pass out of the timber and wait for him. The horse promptly obeyed, for he understood the whispered words. Then the youth placed himself directly behind the horse, ready to fight off any and all assailants, and followed the steed, thus forming his rear guard.

Between Deerfoot and the camp fire loomed the form of an Assiniboine warrior. His sensitive ear had heard the soft neigh, and even the low voice of Deerfoot. He knew that a thief was in the grove—he must have thought he was a Nez Perce—and was making off with Whirlwind, who was held in higher esteem than all the other horses together.

The Shawanoe saw that a fight was inevitable. He passed his rifle to the right hand, over whose arm his blanket was resting, and drew his hunting knife. Even in that crisis the chivalry of the Shawanoe would not allow him to take full advantage of the situation. He could have struck down his enemy without the least risk to himself. He chose rather to give his antagonist warning.

"Dog of an Assiniboine!" he muttered in the Blackfoot tongue. "The Shawanoe fears you not!"

The warrior leaped forward like a crouching tiger. He had caught sight of the lithe form in the faint glow of the firelight, and he assailed it with all the vicious vigor of his nature. The lightning-like blow of his knife made a hissing sound as it cut the air and buried its point in the blanket which Deerfoot thrust forward to receive it. Then the Shawanoe delivered *his* blow. Enough said.

Brief as was the terrific encounter, it occurred too close to camp for the other Assiniboines to remain in doubt for a moment. Moreover, when the victim of the Shawanoe's prowess went down not to rise again he uttered an ear-splitting screech which echoed through the grove.

Deerfoot turned and ran among the trees after Whirlwind. From some cause the stallion had changed his direction and was waiting on the edge of the wood several rods from where his master emerged. The latter glanced hastily around in the gloom without seeing him. He uttered a low signal which the horse instantly obeyed, and with another neigh of delight trotted to his master.

Deerfoot was about to vault upon his back, but hesitated. The sounds indicated that the whole five Assiniboines had rushed to the spot and were already within arm's reach of master and stallion. They would be so near when Whirlwind made his dash that they would fire a volley which was certain to kill one or the other, and not unlikely both rider and animal.

Nor could anything be gained by turning at bay and fighting the whole five, though the Shawanoe would not have hesitated to do that had no other recourse been left to him. With that quick perception which approached the marvelous in him he ordered Whirlwind to gallop along the side of the timber and again wait for him. Then Deerfoot dived among the trees as if in fear of the fierce warriors closing in upon him. His aim was to draw the attention of the party from the stallion to himself, and he succeeded.

For three or four minutes he dodged in and out, where in the gloom he could not escape more than one collision with the limbs. The whole party plunged after him. They knew that the audacious stranger had slain one of their number and were determined he should not escape their vengeance, for with him disposed of the black stallion could be recovered at leisure.

All the time that Deerfoot was whisking here and there, leaping to the right and left, and getting forward as fast as he could, he held his knife grasped and ready to use on the instant the emergency arose. He was so handicapped by the obstructions and the darkness that he could do little more than hold his own. His enemies were too near for him to hide himself from them. Had he attempted to do so the whole lot would have descended upon him like an avalanche.

There was no chance to select his route; all he could do was to drive ahead and avoid being driven at bay. He took care not to pass near the fire, where the glow would have betrayed him. He feared his foes would shoot, though everything was so obscured that they were likely to wait in the hope of capturing him or gaining a fairer aim.

A faint lighting up in front showed that he was nearing the edge of the wood. Two bounds carried him clear, and then, with the utmost speed of which he was capable, he ran along the margin to a slight turn in the conformation of the grove, when he leaped out into the open air and was off with as great fleetness as he displayed on the home-stretch in his race with Ralph Genther, after the turkey shoot at Woodvale.

By his dodging and trickery he had gained an important start, but not enough to put him beyond sight of the Assiniboines, who debouched from the timber at the moment the form of the Shawanoe was fast dissolving in the gloom. They were fleet of foot, and in the belief that they could speedily run the fugitive to earth they made after him. Hardly had the singular race opened when the astounded pursuers saw no fugitive before them! He had been swallowed up in the darkness like an arrow launched from a powerful bow. The Assiniboines must have come to the belief that whoever the stranger was he knew how to run. You and I came to that belief long ago.

One of the chagrined pursuers fired in the direction of the flying fugitive. The bullet probably passed within fifty feet of him, certainly not near enough for Deerfoot to hear the whistle of the missile.

The Shawanoe was too wise to maintain his flight in a direct line, for there was no saying how long his enemies would hunt for him. He made a wide detour to the right and passed around the head of the lake, moving as silently as a shadow and issuing no call to Whirlwind to join him. Reaching the point he had in mind he stopped, peered around in the gloom and carefully located himself. Then he placed his thumb and forefinger between his teeth and pierced the stillness with that peculiar whistle which could have been heard a mile away.

Meanwhile, if we can believe that animals are capable of reasoning, Whirlwind must have had some uncomfortable thoughts. He was listening for the next orders of his master and could make nothing of the tumult going on near him. He would have been eager to lend a helping hand, or, rather, hoof, but did not know how to lend it. He might make matters worse by the attempt. He had received his commands and it only remained for him to obey them.

While thus waiting, the Assiniboine leader—he who claimed him as his particular property—assumed form in the starlight and drew near. Whirlwind snuffed suspiciously. He could not understand matters, but he had seen his master and comrade and resented any impertinence from others.

The Assiniboine hurried up and extended one hand to grasp the forelock of the stallion, in order to lead him back to his place on the other side of the camp. At that moment the signal of Deerfoot rang out.

Perhaps the Assiniboine suspected the meaning of the call, for he darted forward and seized the forelock. Whirlwind instantly reared, and with a single blow of his hoof knocked the red man senseless. He did not kill him, but it is safe to conclude that when the Assiniboine regained his senses he knew a good deal more than he ever knew before.

The waiting Shawanoe heard the sound of hoofs, and a minute later saw the form of the stallion as he galloped up and paused with his nose thrust forward, asking for another caress.

He received it and in his mute way expressed his own pleasure at being with his master again. The danger was not yet over, and the Shawanoe deferred further petting until the opportunity was more fitting. Resting one hand upon the neck of the stallion he leaped lightly astride of him, still keeping the blanket about his own shoulders, for the night was keen and the horse did not need the protection.

Whirlwind yearned to stretch his limbs and speed away with his master on his back. But it would have been unsafe. After leaving the vicinity of the lake the country was rough, and in the darkness the surest-footed horse was liable to fall. Moreover, there was no need of haste.

So the stallion passed out into the night at his usual graceful walk, while his rider for the time listened and peered into the darkness behind him for sound or sight of the Assiniboines who would have given much for a chance to revenge themselves upon the daring youth that had outwitted them.

At the end of half an hour Deerfoot slipped from the back of his steed and pressed his ear to the earth. If the Assiniboines were following and were near he would learn the fact through this better conductor of sound. He heard nothing and once more vaulted upon Whirlwind.

Relieved for the time of all cause for fear, Deerfoot now gave grateful attention to the proud stallion that was bearing him southward. He first tested his recollection of the words of command which he had taught him, and which you will remember were in a peculiar language known only to the two. Whirlwind proved his excellent memory by promptly responding to every order addressed to him. Then the Shawanoe guided him by pressure of his knees, and by a certain manner of striking the heels of his moccasins against his sides. The result could not have been more satisfactory.

"Whirlwind is a bad horse," said Deerfoot, feeling that it was time to have a little sport with him. "He ran away from Deerfoot on purpose. If he had had any sense he would have left the Assiniboines and set out to find Deerfoot instead of making Deerfoot travel so far to find him."

It would be absurd to pretend that a horse, even with the rare intelligence of Whirlwind, could grasp the meaning of these words. However, he understood the sharp pinch which his master gave him on the side of his neck, followed by a brisk slap with his hand. The stallion reached his head around and nipped at the leg of Deerfoot, who drew it back and flipped the nose of the animal.

Then Whirlwind flung his head around his other shoulder and snapped at the leg on that side, which was hardly snatched out of the way in time to escape. Deerfoot gently smote the nose to remind the steed that with all his strength and wisdom the youth was still his master. Thus they parried and played and plagued each other until Deerfoot, with that curious refinement of cruelty which we often show to those we love most, pretended to be offended.

"If Whirlwind wishes to bite Deerfoot he may do so."

And to show he meant what he said he reached forward and placed his hand between the lips of the horse. The latter instantly opened his jaws, so as to inclose the hand with his teeth. A slight effort would have crushed the fingers out of all semblance of symmetry and beauty. Whirlwind did bring his jaws nearly together, but took good care that the pressure was not sufficient to harm a fly.

Deerfoot's heart smoke him. He could not stand this cruelty to as true a friend as ever lived. Resting his rifle across his thighs, so as to leave his hands free, he leaned forward, and, inclosing the satin neck in his grasp, gave the noble creature as fervent an embrace as wooer ever gave to sweetheart.

"Deerfoot loves Whirlwind, and his heart would have been sad all his life if he had not found him. None shall take him away from Deerfoot again. Deerfoot knows that we shall meet in that land that our Father is saving for those who do His will, and then Deerfoot and Whirlwind shall hunt and roam the forests and prairies forever."

If the meaning of the words was vague to the stallion, he could not mistake the meaning of the embrace and the reposing of the side of the Shawanoe's face in the luxuriant mane. He was fully repaid for the indignities he had suffered and the grief that had come to him because of the separation of the two. Had Whirlwind been able to put his ideas in words it is conceivable that he would have reproached the Shawanoe for deserting and leaving him among strangers. Had he not done so, no search with its attendant dangers would have been forced upon the youth.

And had this rebuke been given to Deerfoot, surely he would have admitted the justice of the charge, for we know how he reproached himself for his conduct. But we blame others for ills which we know are caused by ourselves, and we chide unjustly those whom we love most, knowing all the time how unjust we are, and that if we loved less the reproof would not be given at all.

CHAPTER VII.
A MISHAP.

So Deerfoot the Shawanoe rode into the night, his heart aglow with gratitude because of the success of his venture. Whirlwind was his and he felt no misgiving over losing him again, and the steed himself would fight against recapture.

The animal kept to a walk, for to go faster would have been imprudent if not dangerous. He was not traveling over the course followed by Deerfoot in threading his way to the Assiniboine camp. The road was rough and strange to both horse and rider. All that the youth knew of a certainty was that he was journeying southward. He could tell that much by observing the stars that had served him so often as a compass.

Nor was there any necessity for haste. It was impossible for the Assiniboines to trail him until the sun appeared in the sky, when Whirlwind would easily leave the fleetest of their ponies out of sight. So no fear remained in the heart of the dusky youth. Speaking now and then to the animal, patting his neck and shoulder, or playfully pinching the glossy skin, he rode onward for several hours. He was not in need of sleep, and Whirlwind had been given nearly a whole day of rest. It was no task therefore for either to maintain the journey.

Deerfoot's intention was to ride until midnight, when the two would rest, resuming their journey at sunrise and pushing hard until they reached the villages of the Blackfeet. It was late when the stallion splashed through a small brook at the foot of a ridge, where Deerfoot decided to dismount for the remainder of the night. Slipping from the back of the horse he pressed his ear to the earth, but heard nothing to cause him disquiet. If the Assiniboines were hunting for him they were too far off to cause concern.

While Deerfoot was thus employed, Whirlwind stood as motionless as a statue, waiting for his commands. The Shawanoe was in the act of rising to his feet when the steed emitted the slightest possible sniff. He was looking toward the top of the ridge immediately in front, standing like a pointer dog, with his ears pricked forward and head high in air.

Glancing in the same direction, Deerfoot saw the figure of a buck that had come up the other side of the ridge and halted on the crest, as if he scented something amiss. He could not see the two below him, but his own form was thrown into relief against the starlit sky. The beautiful creature with the branching horns, the delicate ears, the shapely head and body, looked as if stamped in ink in the dim star-gleam.

Deerfoot touched the shoulder of Whirlwind as a warning for him to keep still. The intelligent animal maintained his statue-like pose, and the youth began stealing toward the buck, his cocked rifle grasped with both hands and ready to bring to a level and fire on the instant. The space between the two was fifty or sixty yards, which would have been nothing by daylight. The youth wished to decrease it as much as he could because of the darkness, so as to run no risk of missing his aim.

It may not sound poetical, but it is only simple fact that with the sight of the buck unconscious of his danger the dominant emotion of the Shawanoe was a sense of ravening hunger. It was a long time since he had partaken of food and his appetite was worthy of Victor Shelton. He meant that that buck should fill the aching void that vexed him.

A phantom gliding over the ground would have given out no more noise than was made by the moccasins of the Shawanoe; but the timid animal snuffed danger and wheeled to dash away. At the instant of doing so, Deerfoot fired, sending the ball into the body just back of a fore leg. The *cervus* species rarely or never fall, even when stricken through the heart, knowing which, Deerfoot dashed up the slope, knife in hand, and made after the wounded buck, which could be heard threshing among the stones and underbrush. He was still floundering and running when overtaken by the youth, who quickly ended his suffering.

The next act of Deerfoot was to reload his rifle, after which he cut a goodly piece from the side of the game and carried it back to where Whirlwind was waiting. The venison was washed and dressed, after which the youth groped about for fuel with which to start a fire. This proved quite a task, but he succeeded after a time, and then made one of the most substantial meals he had eaten in a long while. When it was completed hardly a fragment was left, and he felt he was provided for in the way of nourishment for a day or two to come, though he saw no reason to fear any such deprivation of food.

The Shawanoe could never forget his caution. While there was little probability of any of the Assiniboines being in the neighborhood, yet it was possible there were, and it might be they had observed the twinkle of the fire he had kindled and then allowed to die out. He remounted his horse and headed more to the westward, for he had a long way to travel to reach the Blackfoot country on the other side of the Rocky Mountains.

The youth was riding forward, glancing to the right and left, on the lookout for a suitable place for camping, when he noticed that while the ground over which he was passing was more level than usual, a high ridge loomed up on the left, rising in some places to a height of several hundred feet. After a time a similar formation appeared on the right. This showed that he was passing through a valley-like depression, but he had gone a comparatively short distance when he observed that the two mountain ranges, if such they might be considered, gradually converged. He turned to the left and at the base of the ridge dismounted.

"Here we will stay for the rest of the night," he said to Whirlwind. "Deerfoot feels that hard work is before us and it is wise to save our strength."

Since there was no saddle or bridle to be taken from the stallion, his master turned him loose, first kissing his nose and affectionately patting his neck. The horse wandered off a few steps to spend the hours by himself, while the youth laid his blanket on the ground and wrapped himself in it. No water was near, nor was there enough grass growing for Whirlwind to crop, but neither cared for a little thing like that.

Deerfoot slept soundly till roused by the licking of his cheek by his faithful friend, who was standing at his head and looking down in his face as revealed in the dim morning light. The night was gone and it had brought no alarm to either.

Casting aside the blanket, Deerfoot sprang to his feet and surveyed his surroundings.

That which first attracted his attention was the convergence of the massive walls to the southeast. Less than half a mile away they came within a hundred feet of each other, thus forming one of the cañons that are common in mountainous countries. The question which Deerfoot asked himself was whether it was probable the two joined. If so, he was entering a pocket from which he would be forced to withdraw. The middle of the valley showed that at certain times, perhaps when the snows melted, a stream coursed its way through the cañon, but the water came from the front and flowed toward the horseman into the open country to the rear. Had it taken the opposite course there would have been no hesitation on his part, for he would have known that an outlet was in advance through which Whirlwind could pass. On the other hand, it might be that the ridges united and the torrent had its source in the water which poured over the rocks at the head. If this proved to be the fact, Deerfoot would be obliged to retreat and make a change of course.

His belief was that the ridges did not join and it was therefore prudent for him to go on. Two causes led him to this conclusion: the ground was favorable for the hoofs of his horse, and the course of the cañon was the direction he wished to follow. It was a small matter anyway, for an hour or two loss of time could make no special difference. He spoke to Whirlwind, who stepped off with his usual proud stride. Now that daylight had come and the ground was inviting, the steed of his own accord broke into an easy gallop, which his rider did not check.

Arriving at the farthest point visible at the moment of starting, Deerfoot found that though the walls drew somewhat closer they did not meet for at least a half mile in front, where again a change of course hid the actual truth. He was now following the black, sandy bed of a stream, packed so hard that it gave an ideal floor for a horse's hoofs.

The Shawanoe had not reached the turn in the cañon when he made an alarming discovery. Looking to the rear he discovered fully a dozen horsemen coming toward him on a walk. They were probably a half mile off, and no doubt were pursuing him. He would not have felt any misgiving but for the instant suspicion that these Indians were Assiniboines and the other division of the party from whom he had retaken Whirlwind. They must have recognized the black stallion, and, if so, of course knew he had been captured by the Nez Perce, as they supposed him to be. On no other supposition could their action be explained.

Without checking his steed, Deerfoot turned and pointed his glass at the red men. One glance was sufficient. They were Assiniboines, and no doubt those for whom the other group were waiting in the grove miles distant.

Where they had come from with such suddenness was more than the Shawanoe could guess. It mattered naught since they were there, and his situation was not only unpleasant, but likely to prove dangerous. If the cañon closed he was fairly caught and would have to make a desperate fight to extricate himself. If it was open in front he had little to fear.

He spoke to Whirlwind, who instantly increased his speed. The Assiniboines seemed to make no effort to lessen the distance between themselves and the fugitive. This looked bad, for it indicated that the Shawanoe was riding toward a shut door and would fall into their power like ripe fruit shaken from a limb.

When Deerfoot reached the next curve in the cañon he perceived that only a little way in front it curved again. He decided at once to settle the doubt in his mind, for, if the cañon was a blind one, every rod of advance added to his danger. The walls drew steadily nearer and he began to fear that they really met not far off. If obliged to turn back he should do so without further delay.

Checking Whirlwind he slipped to the ground and ran to the side of the ravine. He left his blanket on the back of the horse, and leaned his rifle against the base of the rocks, up which he began climbing with the nimbleness of a sailor ascending the rigging of a ship. His intention was to reach the level ground above, from which he could gain a view that would tell him whether it was safe to go any farther into the cañon or whether he must make instant retreat.

From the foot of the mountain wall to the top was fully forty feet, and it was perpendicular all the way; but the face was so rugged that he went up without trouble, only turning a little to the right now and then to gain a better support for his hands and feet. The stallion stood motionless and watching him with what must have been wondering interest.

As he ascended Deerfoot glanced down the ravine and saw the Assiniboines still coming with their horses on a walk. This pointed to the probability that the Shawanoe had really entered a pocket and his enemies saw no need of haste, since they felt sure of their victim. And yet with all his acumen the Shawanoe erred in explaining the deliberation of his pursuers.

At last the agile climber reached the upper edge of the ravine, and it only remained for him to lift himself a foot farther to gain the view which would reveal the truth of the situation. He extended his hand upward to secure the grip that was to raise his head above the level. As he did so he rested it on something cold and soft, which he instantly recognized as a coiled rattlesnake.

Deerfoot shared the shivering disgust which nearly every person feels for crawling reptiles. Nothing was so hideous to him as the *crotalus*, and when he caught sight of one he rarely allowed it to escape. An electric shock thrilled through him as he snatched back his hand in time to avoid the sting, for the snake must have been as much astonished as he by its disturbance. In the horror of the contact the Shawanoe forgot everything else for the instant, and letting go his hold, dropped to the bottom of the gorge.

He realized his mishap the instant it took place and tried desperately to seize some obstruction that would check his descent, but could not do so. He struck the bottom of the cañon, landing on both feet, with a twinge of pain that was like a dagger thrust in his ankle.

But brief as was Deerfoot's descent, he had seen something terrifying while it was going on. The rattlesnake so rudely disturbed as it lay in coil (though it sometimes strikes when not in that position), darted its gaping mouth at the hand which flashed out of its reach. Strange as it may seem, it was lying on the very edge of the gorge, so close indeed that the blow which struck vacancy carried it over, and it came tumbling, looping and writhing after Deerfoot, at whose feet it fell, bruised and stunned by the impact. Before it could strike again he had seized his rifle and crushed out its life.

The excitement of the moment sustained him, but with the blow he sank to the ground as if shot through the heart. His left ankle had been severely wrenched and could not support an ounce of his weight. The pain was so intense that but for his iron will he would have swooned. With wonderful pluck and self-control he carefully raised himself and stood on the right foot, with the other leg bent at the knee and its foot held clear of the ground. A red-hot needle driven into and through the ankle could not have caused more agony.

But though his face and compressed lips were pale, not a murmur of complaint escaped him. Looking up at his steed he said, with his old, winning smile:

"Will Whirlwind take care of Deerfoot, for he cannot take care of himself?"

CHAPTER VIII.
ENEMIES AND FRIENDS.

The black stallion knew his master was in trouble. Stepping forward he thrust forward his nose and licked his face. Deerfoot rested one arm on his mane, the other hand holding his rifle. Then Whirlwind, without a word, kneeled on one knee, so as to lower his shoulders. With a single hop the young Shawanoe leaped upon his back and the steed immediately stood on all-fours.

"Now, my friend, show them what you can do in the way of running."

The incident had taken only a few moments, but brief as was the time it had allowed the Assiniboines to decrease the space between them and the Shawanoe. Singular as it seemed, they still failed to hurry. They held their horses at a walk, and Deerfoot for the first time began to suspect the truth.

Whirlwind was off with the speed of the wind. His motion gave pain to the rider, but it was less than when he stood with one foot on the ground. So long as he had the steed under him he felt little cause for fear.

The theory which had suddenly assumed shape in the mind of Deerfoot was that the pursuers wished to hold him in the ravine while another party passed around to the other entrance. He would thus be placed between two fires and his position made tenfold more perilous than ever. It may be said that if this trick succeeded the doom of both Deerfoot and Whirlwind would be sealed.

And it was precisely the stratagem which the Assiniboines had attempted.

It will now be understood why the Shawanoe sent his steed flying up the gorge at such a tremendous burst of speed that he rapidly drew away from the group behind him. He meant to get out of the ravine before he was shut off in front. No doubt longer remained that it was open at no great distance in advance.

The space was less than a third of a mile after making the last turn. Deerfoot would have been glad had it been greater, for that much more opportunity would be given for the use of the stallion's fleetness.

The Shawanoe descried the open door. The walls fell away, leaving an interval of a hundred yards between, the bottom of the ravine slightly ascended, the ridges gradually dropped to the level of the earth, and the country was spread out as before he rode into the cañon the night previous.

From the back of the flying steed Deerfoot kept his eye on the space, expecting every moment to see the other Assiniboines dash into view and sweep down upon him. He had fixed his line of action. He would charge straight at them, even if they numbered a dozen, using first his rifle and then his knife, should a chance present itself to bring the latter into play.

With every bound of Whirlwind the hopes of his rider rose. It looked as if the race had been won by the superb stallion. A few more strides and all his enemies would be thrown to the rear.

The next moment Whirlwind burst out of the ravine into the open country, and in the same instant came face to face with another horseman. He was the Assiniboine chieftain, who alone had ridden hard along the side of the cañon on the ground above, in order to head off the flying fugitive, and had arrived just in time to do so. He scorned to take any companion with him, for he feared no living man and was sure of overcoming the audacious stranger that had roused his fury.

The Assiniboine must have heard the thunder of the approaching hoofs, for he had checked his own horse, on which he sat awaiting the appearance of the Shawanoe. When the latter caught sight of his face he had his rifle at his shoulder and was in the act of pressing the trigger.

Deerfoot saw he had no time to use his own weapon, for quickly as he might aim it the other would be discharged first. In the language of the modern West, the Assiniboine "had the drop" on the Shawanoe.

There was but one thing to do, and Deerfoot did it in the twinkling of an eye. He flung his body to the other side of his steed, sustaining himself by bending his toes over the base of the stallion's neck. When I add that the foot with which he performed this remarkable bit of horsemanship was the one with the sprained ankle, you may faintly imagine the wrenching torture he suffered. Only by a superhuman effort did he keep control of his senses.

The Assiniboine fired at the moment of the lightning-like shift of position, and Deerfoot heard the zip of the bullet as it sped across the space covered less than a second before by his body.

There is a lurking devil in the most saintly disposition, and that which slumbered in the breast of the young Shawanoe now flamed to a white heat. Swinging back to the upright posture he called:

"Now, Whirlwind, run him down!"

"Now, Whirlwind, Run Him Down."

The stallion felt the pressure of the knees, understood the command, and ablaze with rage, charged like a cyclone for the other horse. In a flash he crashed into the animal, hurling him sidelong to the earth and rolling him completely over from the terrific force of the impact.

But his rider was a fine horseman and leaped to the ground before the collision. Whirling about he faced the Shawanoe, with knife drawn, for there was no time to reload his gun.

He was now at the mercy of Deerfoot, whose weapon was loaded. But for the disabled limb he would have leaped to the earth and assailed the other. He would have done the same had there been two enemies before him; he would have done the same had there been three; but he was not the fool to engage in a fight when he had but a single leg to stand upon.

The panic-stricken horse, having clambered to his feet, dashed away. Whirlwind assumed his statue-like pose and Deerfoot brought his rifle to a level, with the Assiniboine staring into the muzzle.

The fight had been of the cyclone order, but, brief as it was, Deerfoot had become himself again. He was the Christian who could not shed the blood of one that was unable to defend himself, even though that one was his deadly enemy.

The Assiniboine had dropped his gun when assuming his position at bay, and it lay several feet away on the ground. Lowering his own weapon, Deerfoot pointed after the fleeing horse and said sternly in the tongue of the Blackfeet:

"Run! run after the horse!"

The gesture, as much as the words, explained the command. It was so unparalleled, so utterly unexpected, that the Assiniboine stood in a daze. Deerfoot knew that the report of the gun would speedily bring the warriors to the spot, and there was not a minute to spare. He repeated his order more sharply than before and accompanied it with a threatening lifting of his gun to a level.

The other could not misunderstand the significance of voice and gesture. He stepped forward to pick up his rifle.

"Stop!" shouted the Shawanoe, before the other could stoop. "Leave it where it is! Follow the horse."

The hammer of the leveled rifle was at full cock. Still unable fully to comprehend all that had taken place, the chieftain faced about and broke into a lope after his horse, which acted as if it would keep up its pace for the remainder of the day.

Deerfoot waited till the chief had gone a hundred paces, when heading the other way he gave the word to Whirlwind, whom, however, he held down to a walk. The rider wished to witness developments.

Looking back he saw the Assiniboine motionless and gazing after him with emotions that can hardly be imagined or described. He stood thus for a minute, when he started on a run to recover his rifle from where it lay on the ground. Just before reaching the spot the party of horsemen emerged from the mouth of the cañon and paused while their leader rejoined them.

It would be interesting to know how he squared matters with his warriors. It would have required a vivid imagination and a genius in the way of invention to explain how it was his horse was just vanishing in the distance; how the chief was in the act of recovering his weapon, and more than all, how it came about that the youthful warrior of a strange tribe, who had already slain one Assiniboine—though that was yet unknown to this party—was riding leisurely off on the back of the special pet of the chieftain. If the Assiniboine was wise he made a clean breast of it, and insisted that the dusky stranger was a marvel in his way whom it was exceedingly unwise to push into a corner.

The chagrin of the Assiniboine party was not soothed by the action of Deerfoot, who, having spared the life of an enemy, felt himself justified in "rubbing it in," so to speak. He faced Whirlwind toward the group, held him motionless, and, swinging his rifle over his head, indulged in a series of tantalizing shouts that were anything but soothing to the chief and his friends.

How they ached to get the terrible young warrior into their power! What exquisite vengeance they would have wreaked upon him!

But such bliss was impossible. They knew what speed the black stallion possessed, and it was not supposable that his rider meant to challenge all of them to combat. So they maintained a glum silence as he rode from view.

Meanwhile, Deerfoot found he must give attention to the ankle, whose condition had been aggravated by the fight with the Assiniboine leader. It was much swollen and the pain was torturing. Still his bravery and self-command prevented anything in the nature of murmuring. In truth, he would have suffered death without outcry.

The remarkable youth found a strange consolation. He was familiar with the story of the Saviour's death on the cross and remembered the nails that were driven through the hands and feet.

"*He* suffered from four wounds, besides having a spear thrust into his side. Deerfoot has only one hurt in his foot and that does not bleed. *He* had the weight of the world's guilt crushing his heart. What are Deerfoot's sufferings compared with His? It is my Father's will and therefore the heart of Deerfoot is glad."

Failing to see a sign of strangers in the neighborhood, the Shawanoe drew Whirlwind down to a walk and halted at the first mountain stream, which happened to be no larger than the one where he had broiled his supper the night before.

The moment Whirlwind saw that his master wished to dismount he sank upon both knees. His sympathetic act touched Deerfoot, who, stepping carefully upon the well limb, patted the neck of the steed and thanked him.

"Deerfoot would be helpless but for Whirlwind. They must now stick together as never before."

Hopping to the brook the youth slipped off his moccasin and removed the stocking. The swollen ankle was as sensitive as a boil. Dipping the stocking in the icy water he rang it almost dry and rubbed the limb, gently at first and then more vigorously until it was in a glow. This was soothing and gave partial relief, but much pain remained. An injury of that nature takes a long time to subside.

Having never suffered from illness or wounds, the Shawanoe was without any remedy at command, nor did he know aught of the many medicaments which his race, as well as the white people, use. Had the hurt been a simple cut or wound he would have given it no heed, but his sprain forced itself upon his notice.

He finished rubbing the ankle and carefully drew on the stocking, with Whirlwind sympathetically watching him, and doubtless longing for some method of giving relief. I wonder whether the creature recalled that day, many weeks before, when his young master rubbed his injured knee so tenderly and ministered to him until he had fully recovered. We cannot fathom the mysteries of the brain in animals of a high order of intelligence, and it is not for us to deny that such might have been the fact.

Suddenly the stallion turned toward a pile of rocks to the left and emitted his faint, warning neigh. Deerfoot was up in a twinkling, despite the additional suffering caused by his action, and seized his rifle resting near. As he did so an Indian appeared from behind the rocks and came toward him. A glance showed him to be the dwarf with whom Deerfoot had had his singular meeting when journeying northward.

The red man of short stature took long wabbling strides, made numerous gestures and grimaces and rapidly uttered words, not one of which was understood by the Shawanoe. Still chattering, gesticulating and grinning he came forward, without heeding the black steed, flung his long bow to the ground, and kneeling down, gently lifted the foot of Deerfoot, who had not yet drawn on his moccasin. The visitor saw that the limb was injured and tenderly rested the foot upon his knee, the owner thereof making no objection, gently turned down the stocking and spent a minute or two in inspecting the swollen ankle. Then with a sympathetic aspiration he slowly stroked it with his hand. In doing so he drew downward each time and never rubbed the surface upward.

There is something in magnetism, and Deerfoot was sure of a slight cessation of the pain, though the relief was not marked. When the caressing had been repeated a number of times, the dwarf softly laid the foot on the ground and rose to his feet. Another vigorous discharge of unintelligible words followed, and he wabbled rapidly off beyond the rocks from behind which he had come a short time before.

Since he left his bow lying on the ground where he had flung it, Deerfoot knew he had gone in quest of some remedy and would soon return. He therefore kept his seat on the ground and patiently awaited the other's coming.

In a few minutes the dwarf reappeared, bearing in his hand a bunch of green leaves. The twigs were pinnated, and at the base of each leaflet, where it joined the common peticle, was a single crimson berry, resembling the common wintergreen, but the genus was unknown to the Shawanoe, though he knew something of medicinal herbs.

Dividing the twigs with their leaves and berries into halves, the good Samaritan laid one pile on the ground, pointing to it, and still chattering. Deerfoot knew he wished to direct his attention to the healing plant, and he nodded his head to signify he understood and would remember his request.

Then, as deftly as a girl, the dusky friend picked the berries from the twigs in the other bunch. They filled the palm of one hand, which he held out for Deerfoot to inspect. The Shawanoe nodded again. The other wabbled back to the rocks, but did not pass out of sight. Picking up a bit of stone, he began crushing the berries upon a projection of the rocks. It took but a brief time to turn them into a yellow, sticky mass which emitted a slightly aromatic odor. Returning to the patient, he skillfully spread the poultice on several of the larger leaves, laid them over and around the swollen ankle, and then, as gently as a mother with her babe, drew the stocking over it, so as to hold the poultice in place.

Deerfoot leaned back, resting his body on his elbows, and heaved a long, grateful sigh. The relief was bliss itself. For a minute or two he believed the injury was fully healed, but a slight movement of the foot proved that this was not the fact. Nevertheless, the effect of the crushed berries was magical. As he looked up in the homely, twisted countenance, his expression spoke his gratitude. The dwarf grinned. The language of thankfulness needs no interpreter.

Deerfoot came to the upright posture, and, reaching forward, took one of the stranger's hands in his own and patted it, murmuring his thanks.

The dwarf pointed to the twigs and berries remaining untouched and said something, which was made clear by the rapid flitting of his forefinger from them to the wounded member. The meaning was plain. The patient was to use them as the others had been used. Deerfoot signified in his usual way that he understood the direction.

The dwarf stood for a few minutes silent, with his eyes on the face of the Shawanoe seated before him. Then he spoke again, and Deerfoot would have given much to have understood the words, but he could not form the remotest idea of their meaning. The visitor stopped and picked up his bow from the ground, turned and swung with his awkward gait up the slight slope, passed from sight behind the pile of rocks, and the Shawanoe never saw or heard of him again.

CHAPTER IX.
IN THE ROCKIES.

There was wonderful virtue in the remedy used by the dwarf Indian. You and I know that in many a mountaineer's cabin and barbarian's wigwam are found curatives which surpass anything known to what we call medical science. The proofs of this fact are too numerous to be questioned.

As Deerfoot rode away with Whirlwind on a walk, he knew his hurt had been greatly benefited. With his foot hanging, the flow of blood downward tended to increase the pain, but there was not only less of it than at any time since his mishap, but it was perceptibly decreasing. The swelling was going down, for the stocking was becoming looser. He timidly tapped the ribs of the stallion with his heel and was delighted to find it caused less of a twinge than he expected.

At the first water he paused, but would not allow Whirlwind to kneel to help him dismount. He let himself down rather gingerly and did not suffer therefrom. At the side of the little stream he examined his injury. The swelling was markedly less and he was able to press it without wincing. He had brought away the surplus berries, but, instead of using them, moistened the old binding and replaced it. It might be that he would not be able to find more of the remedy, and it was prudent to husband the supply. Observant as he was, he did not recall ever having seen the shrub growing, and was certain it was not found in Ohio or Kentucky.

One potent factor in the rapid recovery of the Shawanoe must not be overlooked; that was his own superb health and condition. You need not be reminded that when anything goes amiss with us physically, nature sets to work at once to right it, and the most that medical skill can do is to sit by and watch for contingencies and give assistance as opportunity offers, which is less frequent than many think. A system that has not been weakened by dissipation or the violation of the laws of health will do wonders in the way of repairing disease or injury.

It was not yet noon when Deerfoot became so hopeful and curious that he suddenly slipped from the back of his horse without checking his walk.

Whirlwind must have been startled, for he instantly stopped and turned his head to learn what it meant.

"Don't worry," said his master with his familiar chuckle. "Deerfoot is almost well and will soon be himself again."

He ventured to bear a part of his weight on the weak leg. It caused a twinge, and he instantly shifted to the other foot, but with the transference of weight the pain departed, which was one of the best of signs.

The days of miracles passed long ago, and with all the virtues that may linger in the Thomsonian system of medicine, no possibility existed of the Shawanoe regaining the full use of his limb for several days to come. None the less, his recovery was astonishingly rapid, for, as I have said, his perfect vigor and healthfulness of body greatly aided in such recovery. Added to this was the intelligence he used. While he frequently tested and experimented with the injury, he did not venture too far. Now and then he carefully shifted a part of his weight to his left limb, then he hobbled a few steps, but stopped immediately at the first warning twinge. It may be said he encouraged the ankle to do its best to get well.

It was a little past meridian when he reached a place which showed a considerable growth of grass, and letting himself down to the ground, he told Whirlwind to attend to his own dinner. As for himself, he preferred to wait until nightfall, or the next day. At present all his attention was given to his hurt.

He decided, after inspecting the bandage, to replace it with a new one. He therefore flung the old one aside and mashed the berries and applied them as the dwarf had done. But the injured limb had so decreased in size that the stocking failed to hold it in place. The motion of the horse caused the bandage to slip over the foot. This was remedied by taking some of the threads of fringe from the skirt of his hunting shirt and tying them round the poultice. He expected the increased pressure to hurt, but to his pleased surprise the opposite effect resulted.

It had been in his mind to construct a crude crutch to aid in hobbling around, but he decided not to do so. If his recovery continued without relapse he could do well enough without such aid.

On the journey from the Ohio to the Pacific, as well as during their intimacy in the new State, Deerfoot and Mul-tal-la had talked so much about the home of the latter that the Shawanoe felt himself well informed. A hundred years ago that tribe numbered several thousand, and they lived in villages, some of which were long distances from one another. The country over which they roamed covered thousands of square miles of mountain, prairie and stream. Mul-tal-la described his own village as consisting of more than a hundred lodges, located near the middle of the Blackfoot territory. The tepees were strung along the eastern bank of a stream of considerable size, and was the dwelling-place of Taggarak, the most famous of the Blackfoot war chiefs and the head of the other sachems, most of whom lived in different villages. Deerfoot had formed so clear a picture in his own mind that he believed he could identify the Indian town at first sight, though it might be its resemblance to others would prevent such recognition.

The Blackfoot country lies to the east of the Rocky Mountains, while he was on the west of the stupendous range. It was necessary, therefore, to make his way through and over the backbone of the continent, in order to rejoin his friends. Inasmuch as the land of the Assiniboines was not only farther east, but many leagues to the northward, it will be understood that the party that had tried to run off Whirlwind had ventured on a most extensive raid, which brought them no reward except that of having slain several of Chief Amokeat's Nez Perces.

A requirement for getting through the mountains was an avenue, since the passage could be effected in no other way except by flying, and Deerfoot was not yet ready to try that means.

Using all the woodcraft of which he was master, he spent the remainder of the day in searching for such a pass. He scanned every part of his field of vision, but the day was drawing to a close before anything like success came to him. He had learned that the warriors to the east and west of the Rockies made journeys now and then back and forth. Sometimes these were raiding expeditions, at other times were merely rambles or visits, when the red men proved themselves capable of hospitality and friendship.

These people must be acquainted with the readiest means of travel, and wherever they walked or rode they left inevitable signs to guide others. The sun was still two hours above the horizon when Deerfoot came upon a plainly marked trail, leading almost due east and west. Without hesitation he turned into it. Instead of being a comparatively narrow passage, however, like that traversed by Mul-tal-la and George and Victor Shelton when they thought they were embroiled with the Shoshones, it was two or three miles wide, and even wider in some places. The ground was so depressed that it partook of the nature of a valley, through the middle of which a considerable stream of water had flowed, fed no doubt, as was the rule, by the melting snows and ice of the mountains.

The surface of this pass varied greatly. There were portions where boulders, rocks and ravines seemed to bar all progress, but these obstructions, upon a closer approach, revealed passages which could be easily traversed by horse or animal. Then came long stretches of fairly level land, where grass, trees and shrubbery were abundant. The mountains towered on the right and left, and now and then directly in front, some of the peaks piercing the sky far above the snow line.

Deerfoot would not have dared to attempt this passage but for the proofs that it had been traversed before by others. In fact, shortly after he made the change of direction he came upon a spot where a large party had encamped not long previous. It was too early in the day to halt for the night, and he allowed the stallion to pass on.

An hour later, when casting about for a suitable camping site, he descried an Indian party not far in advance, but a fourth of a mile to the left. While they were using the same pass with himself, they were traversing another portion and pursuing the same direction as he.

Not convinced that it was well to seek their company, the Shawanoe brought his glass to bear and surveyed the motley group that were straggling eastward. The sight was interesting even to him, for the Indians were composed of warriors, squaws, children and pappooses, evidently migrating to a new home. They had eight or ten scraggly ponies, each walking between two poles that served as shafts and extended so far to the rear that they dragged on the ground. Thus they served as runners or crude sleds. Held in place by thongs and crosspieces, the primitive wagon gave a resting place for tired squaws and children, their lazy husbands, or the furs and luggage of the party. The primitive contrivances left a peculiar trail.

The Indians numbered perhaps fifty or three score, and had nothing attractive in their slouching, untidy appearance, which suggested so many dusky tramps on their way to quarters that offered a better opportunity for begging. Deerfoot had no wish to gain a closer acquaintance and kept well to the south, so as to be sure of passing without mingling with the company. As the ground was favorable he put Whirlwind at a moderate gallop.

The dusky strangers showed their keenness of vision by observing the stranger almost as soon as he descried them. He saw several of the warriors who were on foot point toward him. They seemed to expect Deerfoot to come forward, but, when he did not do so, showed no further interest in him.

The wish to keep clear of the uninviting throng caused the youth to ride on until the gathering gloom told him night was at hand. He then saw he had come to another place that had served as a camp for those who had traveled the way before him. There were the little stream of icy water, the rank grass, the scattered undergrowth and the boulders and rocks of every size and variety.

The air was so chilly that Deerfoot began gathering wood for a fire, though he had nothing in the nature of food for an evening meal. I have shown, however, that that was a matter of small account to him. There was more than enough for Whirlwind, who, leaving his master to himself, began edging up the pass, cropping the choicest grass on the way. The Shawanoe had to grope in many places before he collected enough fuel. He heaped a part against the cold bare face of the rock, several paces from the winding brook, whose waters were not only clear, but of the temperature of ice itself.

With his usual deftness, Deerfoot soon had the fire blazing. He had not seen living man or animal since his sight of the migrating Indians, and he did not think it likely he would meet any before morning. The past day and night had been so stirring that the present rest was grateful. He assumed an easy posture, half reclining on his blanket, and, supporting the upper part of his body on one elbow, he drew out his Bible and held it so that the firelight fell on the printed page.

He read for a full hour. Many of the passages were familiar to him, and he could repeat them—as he often did when riding or walking alone—without glancing within the volume. He read some of the chapters a second and third time, dwelling on certain verses, as if to make sure he lost nothing of their wonderful significance and beauty. Finally, he closed the book and placed it back in its usual resting place.

The fire was sinking and he flung more wood on the blaze. Then moving beyond the circle of light, he gathered his blanket about his shoulders, and, finding his ankle free from pain, leaned back against the face of the rock and gave himself over to meditation upon the fascinating and yet awesome mysteries of the Word and of the Author of them all.

Everything favored the sweet, solemn reverie. He was utterly alone, so far as any of his kind was concerned. He could hear the soft impact of Whirlwind's hoof now and then as he shifted his position and continued nibbling the grass. The night wind sighed around the massive rock, fanning the blaze, and sometimes rising to a moan as it careered upward and swirled about the stupendous peaks towering near at hand. Far aloft he caught the faint honk of the wild geese hurrying southward from the Arctic winter that would soon lock the world in its rigid fetters. The dismal howl of a mountain wolf sounded far off in the solitude and seemed to linger tremblingly in the air. The silence was all the more impressive because of these disturbances which belonged to the time and place.

Leaning back against the rugged rock, in which a slight warmth was perceptible from the contact farther away with the blaze, Deerfoot's thoughts drifted to other places, scenes and persons. He recalled his rambles with Ned Preston, Jo Springer, Jim Turner and the quaint negro youth known as "Blossom," when all passed through many stirring experiences, as you learned long since in the "Boy Pioneer Series;" and of Jack Carleton and Otto Relstaub in the "Log Cabin" stories. Fred Linden and Terry Clark were to come later.

Deerfoot had known many men who later gained a place in history. You will recall the high esteem in which he was held by General W. H. Harrison, Governor of Indiana Territory, and afterward President of the United States. It was he who declared, when a Senator in Washington, that he looked upon the young Shawanoe as the greatest Indian in many respects that ever lived, with natural abilities superior to those of the renowned Tecumseh, who, nevertheless, holds the most exalted position in the estimate of those that came after him.

Daniel Boone, the renowned pioneer, regarded the youth highly, while Simon Kenton, himself one of the best judges of men, was as unstinted in his praise as Governor Harrison. The acceptance of Christianity by this remarkable youth shut out forever the political fame and power that he would have assuredly won had he refused the true faith and been an Indian in his traits, tastes and ambitions. But the sweet, soul-satisfying happiness that was always his he would not have exchanged for the highest honors the world can give.

Deerfoot Lost in Reverie by the Camp Fire.

The musings of Deerfoot took a daintier, softer, tenderer tint. His thoughts flew across the thousands of miles of forest, river, mountain and prairie to one whose image was never absent from his heart, and whom he hoped to see again and all in good time call *wife*. He talked to none of her, for the theme was too sacred to be shared with another, but next to his religion it was the sweetest, dearest consolation of his life.

"In the rainbow-tinted forest,
Where the sleepy waters flow,—
Roamed I with a dark-haired maiden,
In an autumn long ago;
And her dimpled hand was resting
Timidly within mine own,
And her voice to mine replying,

In a whispered undertone."

CHAPTER X.
IN THE BLACKFOOT COUNTRY.

One keen, sunny afternoon in autumn, a certain Indian youth executed a war dance among the foothills to the east of the Rocky Mountains. The only spectator of the fantastic performance was a superb black stallion, who, so far as can be judged, found a good deal of entertainment in the sight. It was long before the days of kodaks and their snapshots, which add so much to our enjoyment of everyday incidents.

Although Deerfoot did not waste any time, it took him a fortnight to thread his way through that immense range which ribs the western part of our continent. After using the last of the crimson berries that benefited his sprain so much, he spent several hours in hunting for the herb; but search high and low as much as he might, he not only failed to find it, but was never able to discover the fruit in any part of the West.

On the morning following his first encampment in the mountain pass he found himself strong enough, by using care, to walk upon the hurt ankle. He was too wise to push matters too fast, which fact, added to his perfect physical condition and the effect of the herb, carried him swiftly along the road to recovery. At the end of a week not a trace of lameness remained. He was cured.

His prudence restrained him until he emerged from the mountain proper into the foothills, when, knowing he was as strong as ever, he indulged in the exuberant outburst. Leaving his blanket upon the back of Whirlwind, but holding his rifle in one hand, Deerfoot leaped into the air, spun around first on one foot and then the other, sent his shapely legs flying seemingly in a dozen different directions at the same moment, swung his arms, bent his body, cavorted and made contortions that would have honored a professional acrobat. Not only that, but he punctuated the extravagant display by a series of whoops such as had nerved the Shawanoe warriors many a time to rush into battle.

All this time Whirlwind stood calmly watching the performance. It is reasonable to believe he was interested, and had he possessed the power of laughter he would have thrown back his head and "cracked his sides" at the sight. What a pity that George and Victor Shelton could not have peeped out from some concealment. They would have remembered the picture all their lives.

Only by this grotesque exercise could the young Shawanoe find vent for his overflowing spirits. There is nothing in all the world that can take the place of physical vigor and health—a truth which unnumbered thousands do not realize until too late. Temperance, right living, obedience to the laws of hygiene, and a clear conscience, never fail to bring their reward and to give to this life a foretaste of the blessed one to come.

Deerfoot had chosen an open space, walled in by rocks, boulders and stunted undergrowth for his physical outburst. When the performance had gone on for some time, he danced up to the side of Whirlwind and planted one of his feet against his ribs so sharply that the stallion was forced back for a step. Instantly he wheeled, partly reared and struck at his insulter, but he was so afraid of hitting him that the blow was awkward and missed the Shawanoe by a goodly distance. As he dropped on his feet, Deerfoot darted under his belly and repeated the blow from the other side. The white teeth of the steed snapped within a few inches of the shoulder of the youth, who slapped the nose before it could be withdrawn.

Whirlwind wheeled to face his master, who landed lightly on his back and pounded his sides with his heels. The contest recalled that other struggle between the two, months before on the prairie, when it was a battle royal indeed. But the great difference lay in the fact that the present one was good-natured on both sides, and it is easy to believe that the stallion wished the youth to prove himself once again his master. An intelligent animal loves to obey him who has proved his superiority.

There is no telling all that was done by the Shawanoe. He sharply pinched the glossy hide. He griped the nostrils of the steed as if to shut off his breath, but was too considerate to continue this long, since the horse seems unable to breathe through his mouth. He placed his hand and forearm over the eyes of Whirlwind as if he meant to play blind-man's buff with him. He yanked the forelock and reproached him as being of no account.

The stallion did his part in the way of defense and retaliation, but he was continually handicapped by his dread of hurting his master. And yet it would seem that, recalling that other conflict, he ought to have had no such apprehension, for he had done his best on that occasion to kill the Indian youth, who was not harmed at all, and overcame the creature that possessed ten times his strength.

Whirlwind showed signs of fatigue before Deerfoot did. A comparatively clear path stretched in front. Dropping from the back of the horse, the Shawanoe challenged him to a race. Bounding off at his highest bent, the youth dashed across the country with the speed of the wind. He ran as he did when on the second half of his race with Ralph Genther.

Ah, Whirlwind had him now! No danger of hurting his audacious master, except so far as his feelings were concerned, and the stallion did not spare them. Despite the favorable ground, more than one boulder or bunch of matted undergrowth had to be leaped, and the two went over them like a couple of flying birds. But the steed steadily drew away from the fleet Shawanoe, who at the end of two or three hundred yards, finding himself hopelessly to the rear, gave up.

"Deerfoot is only a child when he races with Whirlwind; have mercy on him."

Hearing his call, the steed ceased his running, wheeled about and waited for his master to come up. Deerfoot patted him affectionately and vaulted upon his back, happy as he could be over the triumph of his matchless animal that was as well pleased as he.

The journey through the Rocky Mountains was accompanied by many interesting experiences which cannot be dwelt upon. It need hardly be said that so peerless a hunter as the young Shawanoe never lacked for food. That region is still a royal one for game, and it was such to a more marked degree a century ago. Antelope, deer, bison and the famous Rocky Mountain sheep were often seen, and when Deerfoot felt the need of the food it was simple sport to obtain it.

One day, while walking in front of Whirlwind, he came upon an enormous grizzly bear that seemed disposed to dispute their way. The stallion trembled with fear, but his master soothed him and prepared for a desperate fight. Deerfoot never killed an animal in wantonness, and, though he did not doubt that he could overcome this colossal terror, he preferred to make a detour of the broad pass and leave him undisputed monarch of the solitude.

But, if the youth showed mercy to animals, he was not so considerate of reptiles—especially when they crawled the earth. He detested a serpent with unspeakable disgust, and believed he was doing good work in reducing, as opportunity presented, the noxious pests. His experience with the rattlesnake which caused his wrenched ankle did not lessen this hatred of the species. When, therefore, a warning rattle told him one afternoon that he had disturbed another of the venomous things beside the path, his enmity flared up. No fear of the Shawanoe being caught unawares, as when climbing the wall of the cañon, for he had slain too many of the reptiles in his distant home not to understand their nature. Whirlwind, like all of his kind, had a mortal dread of every species of serpents, and he showed his timidity the moment the locust-like whirring sounded from the bush at the side of the path the two were following.

Deerfoot caught sight of the hideous reptile, which was evidently gliding over the earth when it detected his approach. It instantly threw itself into coil, and with its flat triangular head upraised and slowly oscillating back and forth, waited for the intruder to come within reach of its deadly fangs.

Deerfoot uttered an expression of astonishment, for it was the largest specimen upon which he had ever looked, and he had seen many of enormous size. He stood for a few minutes, surveying the horrible thing, a single bite from which would have been fatal to man or animal.

It would have been easy to clip off its head with a rifle shot from where he stood, but he scorned to waste powder and ball upon its species. Three stones, almost the size of his fist, did the work effectually. When no semblance of life remained, Deerfoot approached nigh enough to count the rattles. They were twenty-eight in number. The time was near for serpents and bears to take to winter quarters, and the fate of this extraordinary *crotalus* forcibly illustrated the truth that delays are often dangerous.

Several times on the road, Deerfoot met those of his own race. Sometimes they were warriors riding their ponies, and again they were on foot. The Indian seems to be migratory by nature, and many of these families were shifting their homes, apparently in obedience to the yearning for change which is not confined to uncivilized people alone. It is worthy of note that the Shawanoe not once had any trouble with these strangers. They were hospitable and made their meaning known by the universal sign language. Whirlwind could not fail to draw much admiration, and Deerfoot saw more than one envious eye cast on the stallion. It may have been due to the Shawanoe's caution and tact that no attempt was made to rob him of his treasure.

Winter was near, and, though only one or two flurries of snow were encountered, the temperature often sank below the freezing point. Soon after entering the foothills a driving storm of sleet set in which stopped progress on the part of the Shawanoe and his horse. The youth sought out the most sheltered nook he could find among the rocks and kept a fire going. While he felt no discomfort himself, his companion suffered considerably. He often slept on his feet, but now and then lay down. Deerfoot compelled him to share his blanket, and this, with the warmth of the blaze, did much to make the steed comfortable. It was difficult at times for him to obtain grazing, and Deerfoot gave him aid, as he did months before, when suffering from his lamed knee.

Several days later the youth left the side of the stallion and climbed to the top of a rocky elevation, which commanded an extensive view in every direction. His eye had roved over the expanse but a few minutes when it rested on an Indian village that lay a dozen miles to the northeast. Adjusting the spyglass he carefully studied the collection of tepees, which numbered about a hundred, scattered over several acres. At the rear stretched a forest, and in front flowed a large, winding stream that eventually found its outlet in some of the tributaries of the Missouri.

The question with the Shawanoe was whether or not this was the village he was seeking. Since he had never seen it before, and since it was the custom of all Indian tribes to locate near running water, he could not make certain on that point from the description given by Mul-tal-la.

The glass was an excellent one, and through its aid he could discern the figures of people moving aimlessly hither and thither. He saw two men enter a canoe, formed from a hollowed log, and paddle to the other side of the stream, where they stepped out and advanced into a rocky wood. He thought one of these warriors carried a gun and the other a bow, but could not assure himself on that point. At the rear of the village, in a large open space, fully a score of boys and girls were playing with as much vigor as if they were civilized. They seemed to have a ball that was knocked to and fro and chased by the happy contestants, who often tumbled over one another and again were piled up like so many football players.

Knowing he might gaze and speculate for hours without gaining any certain knowledge, Deerfoot was about to lower his instrument when he observed three horsemen emerging from the settlement and riding in Indian file toward him. He decided to go forward and meet them, for they could give the information he was so anxious to obtain.

Within the following hour the Shawanoe, riding Whirlwind, came face to face with the horsemen, whom he recognized from their dress and general appearance as Blackfeet. He saluted and addressed them in their own tongue, causing manifest surprise. They replied to his signs and expressions of good-will and checked their animals to hear what he had to say. Let us interpret the conversation with more than usual freedom.

"Do my brothers belong to the Blackfoot tribe of red men?" asked Deerfoot.

"We are of that tribe," replied the one who acted as leader.

"I come from the Shawanoes, who live a long way toward the rising sun."

"Why does the Shawanoe travel so far from the lodges of his people?"

"I am seeking friends who are with the Blackfeet. They left many moons ago, but parted company with me in the land of the Nez Perces. I am trying to join them. They are two pale-faced lads who have as their guide a good Blackfoot, Mul-tal-la, that has made the long journey to the home of the Shawanoes."

Upon hearing these words the latter turned his head and spoke for several minutes to his companions, but his words were so low that Deerfoot could not overhear them.

"Is Mul-tal-la in the home of my brothers?"

"No," was the response. "He does not live there."

"Where does he live?"

Instead of directly answering this question the Blackfoot leader said:

"He lives in another village. What is the name of his chief?"

"He told me it was Taggarak."

"He is the great war chief of the Blackfeet. There is no sachem or chief like him. His arm is powerful and has slain many Assiniboines and Nez Perces and Shoshones."

"The words of my brothers were told to me long ago by Mul-tal-la. I am sure they are true. Where shall I seek Taggarak?"

The Blackfoot pointed to the northwest.

"Ride that way till night comes and the sun is again overhead, and he will look upon the village of Taggarak and the home of Mul-tal-la."

This was acceptable information, but a vague fear caused Deerfoot to inquire further.

"Have my brothers seen Mul-tal-la since he came home from his long journey?"

"No; we have heard that he has come back, but he did not bring his comrade with him."

"Have my brothers met the pale-faced youths who went to the village of Taggarak?"

"No; we have not seen them, nor have we heard of them."

This was discomforting news, for it would seem that if tidings had come of the return of Mul-tal-la, something also would have been said of his companions, who belonged to another race. Deerfoot asked only a few more questions, when he bade the Blackfeet good-bye and set out to hunt the village of the war chief Taggarak, where, if all had gone well, he would meet Mul-tal-la and the brothers, George and Victor Shelton.

CHAPTER XI.

IN WINTER QUARTERS.

The time has come for us to turn our attention to George and Victor Shelton, who, after parting with Deerfoot, set out for the principal Blackfoot village under the guidance of their old friend Mul-tal-la, a member of that powerful organization of the Northwest.

You will recall that when the little party of explorers were approaching the home of the tribe they met two warriors, who were old friends of Mul-tal-la and lived in the same primitive settlement with him. After Mul-tal-la had made known the sad fate of his companion in the East, an earnest talk took place and the decision was made that it would not only be imprudent but dangerous to the last degree for the Blackfoot to return home, taking with him the first announcement of the deplorable accident that had robbed the tribe of one of its best warriors.

Taggarak, the leading war chief, was a terrible sachem, who, on the principle that has ruled for centuries in China, would put Mul-tal-la to death, even though he was wholly blameless of neglect or wrongdoing. It was agreed that our friends should push on to the westward, and then come back to the Blackfoot settlement, where the Shawanoe and the brothers would spend the winter, resuming their homeward journey with the coming of spring.

This would defer the arrival of Mul-tal-la for two or three months, which his two friends would utilize the best they could. Taggarak would have time for the cooling of his resentful rage, and it was to be hoped that he would appreciate the service of Mul-tal-la, who, young as he was, had proved himself one of the bravest of warriors. The plan was a wise one and it worked well.

The two messengers had a story of absorbing interest to tell. They hinted at the remarkable experience of their comrade among his own race and the white people, hundreds of miles toward the rising sun. They said that when he came to the village he would bring with him a member of the chief tribe of the East and two pale-faced youths, who would honor the Blackfeet by accepting their hospitality for the winter. There was something in this fact that appealed to that chivalric feeling which is never wholly lacking in the most degraded and cruel race. Taggarak had little to say, but the path to his magnanimity had been paved.

One of the chief causes of this relaxation of sternness on his part was the accounts which he heard of the Indian youth. His fleetness of foot, his skill with bow and rifle, his personal daring and prowess, his quickness and strength, his comeliness of face and form, were dwelt upon and pictured in the most glowing language. The chieftain Taggarak's question of the messengers was characteristic, as was their reply.

"Are all the warriors of the Shawanoes like this youth of whom you tell these strange stories?"

"The Shawanoes are no braver than the Blackfeet, but there is none among them like Deerfoot, nor can his equal be found in all the world."

Among those who doubted the truth of the words of the messengers were several aspiring bucks, who secretly resolved never to admit the superiority of the Shawanoe youth in any of the respects named until such superiority had been proved before their eyes.

The curiosity and spirit of hospitality were general among the Blackfeet. Expecting the visitors to spend several months with them, they made preparations for their convenience and comfort. One of the first things undertaken by the two who had met the little party was the building of a tepee or home for them. Mul-tal-la had his own father and mother and would go to their lodge, but it would not have been seemly to place the three guests with anyone else.

It has already been said that the Blackfoot village, which was the main one of the tribe and the dwelling-place of the leading chief, was stretched along the bank of a running stream which was a remote tributary of the Missouri. This river had a rapid current and ran almost due south in front of the village, which lay wholly on the eastern bank. The tepees were more than a hundred in number, and, when Taggarak went on the war path, he had taken more than two hundred warriors from his own town—and they were the flower of the tribe.

To the rear of the settlement was an open space covering several acres. This was not only the children's playground, but was often used by the warriors for their games and athletic exercises. The space was so extensive that at certain seasons of the year the outer portions were covered with rich nourishing grass, which was also abundant in the neighborhood. Nearly every warrior was the owner of a horse, which, when not in use, was allowed to wander and graze at will.

These Indians lived after the manner of their race when removed from civilization, which, as a rule, has proved a greater curse than boon to them. Fortunately they knew nothing of the ruinous "fire water" that was to await the coming of professing Christians and the claimants of a higher culture and civilization. They spent their time mainly in hunting and fishing, sometimes engaging in raids upon other tribes, several of whose grounds lay to the north of the boundary line. When not thus employed they lolled about, like true lords of creation, smoking, drowsing or indifferently watching their squaws, who did all the tilling of the ground and gathering of the scant crops from the rich soil. The Blackfeet lived too far to the eastward to take any part in the salmon fishing which gave employment to so many of their race on the western slope of the Rocky Mountains. The warriors were finely formed, and were held in no little respect and fear by the neighboring red men, most of whom at some time or other had felt the weight of their prowess.

The home for the expected visitors was erected at the extreme northern end of the village, and was separated by fully fifty yards from the next neighbor to the south. About a dozen saplings were planted in the ground so as to form a circle, perhaps fifteen feet in diameter and a little less in height. The tops were tied together, but loosely enough to leave an opening a foot or more across to serve as a chimney. Over the framework thus formed were stretched with no little skill a number of bison furs, with the furry side in. They were stitched together by means of deer sinews and pegged at the bottom, so as to shut out all draught. Thus all the interior walls were brown and shaggy and warm. On the outside of numerous tepees, cured and whitened by the storms, many of the aboriginal artists of the tribe had sketched grotesque figures of men, horses and wild animals.

You will note that the temporary home of our friends was of the most primitive character, and yet all had seen such before and Deerfoot had spent many a day and night in similar ones in the East. At one side a loose bison robe could be lifted, thus serving as a door. When the weather was warm this fold was often fastened back to permit a partial ventilation of the lodge.

In the middle of the space the fire was kindled, the smoke finding escape through the opening in the saplings at the crown of the structure. Despite the care with which the robes were joined together, enough air stole through the crevices to give the necessary draught for the chimney and furnish the occupants comparatively pure sustenance for their lungs.

The bare ground was the only floor to these rude structures, but the blankets and furs served as so many rugs, and the dwellings, with the crackling fire in the center, could be made comfortable even in the depth of the rigorous winters.

At that early day, more firearms than would be supposed were found among the Indian tribes of the Northwest, though naturally the old-fashioned bow and arrow were the main weapon. The flintlocks were gotten by barter with tribes on the other side of the Rockies, who in turn managed to buy them from the few ships that were beginning to trade with the savages about the lower waters of the Columbia. These guns were comparatively few in number, and it is hardly probable that there were a score among the whole tribe. Few as were the firearms, several good marksmen had been developed among the Blackfeet, and they were naturally proud of their skill. When a party engaged in one of their raids, all the muskets were taken with them. But ammunition was used sparingly, for it necessitated long and expensive journeys through the mountains to renew the supply. You remember that Mul-tal-la left home with only his bow and arrow.

The messengers, when spending their brief time with our friends while they were pushing toward the Pacific, heard of that new religion which was professed not only by Deerfoot the Shawanoe, but by his companions. It was so different from the pagan belief that the couple, upon their return to the village, took care to make no mention of it; better to leave that until the arrival of Deerfoot. At the same time the two Blackfeet trembled when they thought of what was almost certain to take place. Taggarak was a fierce heathen who would savagely resent any interference with the crude belief that had belonged to his people from time immemorial. A collision between him and Deerfoot, and perhaps with his companions, was among the certainties of the near future.

Thus everything had been prepared for Mul-tal-la and the Shelton brothers when one afternoon the three rode into the village, with Zigzag the packhorse plodding at the rear of the procession. The arrival made a hubbub of excitement, and it seemed as if the whole settlement—men, squaws and children—gathered clamorously round the horsemen, who dismounted and gazed about them with scarcely less wonder.

The parents of Mul-tal-la remained in their own lodge. They must have been more eager than any to welcome the son that had been gone so long out of their world, but it would have been weakness on their part to hasten to greet him. Besides, he must needs look after the white youths, who had now become more dependent than ever upon him.

The two former acquaintances were among the first to crowd forward to welcome the boys and their old companion. There was no mistake as to the genuineness of *their* pleasure. They told of the quarters awaiting the lads, who, remounting with Mul-tal-la, rode to the new residence erected at the northern extremity of the Blackfoot town, with their guides walking beside their animals.

Mul-tal-la was as stoical as any of his race, though he was yearning to look upon that father and mother who would greet him, and he them, as if they had been parted for only a few hours. Slipping to the ground again, the three took a peep at the interior of the tepee which has already been described to you. The boys expressed their delight and thanked their friends over and over again. Then Mul-tal-la bade them good-bye, promising to call in a short time, after which he lounged away toward his own lodge. On the road he continually encountered his old friends and exchanged greetings and talked with them as if glad of an excuse for delaying his reunion with his parents.

One of the first bits of news imparted to the Blackfoot was that Taggarak was absent on a visit to the farthest village to the north, but was expected soon to return. Mul-tal-la was relieved to hear this, for, despite the assurances of his friends, he dreaded the anger of the terrible chieftain.

When within a hundred yards of his home, which remained closed as if deserted, Mul-tal-la turned into the tepee where dwelt the parents of the companion who had been buried hundreds of miles away. The father sat on a pile of furs at one side of the lodge, stolidly smoking his pipe. His squaw was kneeling in front of the burning wood and trying to blow it into a blaze. They looked up as the visitor drew aside the flap which served as a door. The old warrior removed the long stem from his lips and grunted as he recognized the visitor. The squaw raised her head, saw who the caller was, and resumed blowing the fire, as if she had no interest in what he might say.

Mul-tal-la told briefly the particulars of what the couple already knew, speaking words of praise for the lost one, and saying how sad his heart had been since the dreadful accident that befell his companion.

The father replaced the stem in his mouth and slowly puffed. Once he grunted, but did not speak a word. The mother continued to fill her leathern cheeks with air and to blow upon the fagots that were burning so strongly as not to need any urging. She did not speak nor look up until several minutes after the departure of Mul-tal-la.

CHAPTER XII.
BLACKFOOT CITIZENS.

"Well," said Victor Shelton, "our tramping is through for several months to come, and we may as well settle ourselves for the winter."

"There doesn't seem much to do in the way of settling," returned his brother; "here we are, and here we must stay till spring comes round. I wish it were with us now, for since we have started for the Ohio I have become homesick."

"We'll soon get used to this life and shall feel better when Deerfoot joins us."

They had removed the saddles and bridles from their horses and the pack from the sturdy, faithful Zigzag, and brought them into their new home, after which the animals, including Bug, the property of Mul-tal-la, had been turned loose to browse with the others at the rear of the village. Blankets were spread on the ground at one side of the tepee, to serve as seats and couches, and the other conveniences, which made up most of the burden carried thousands of miles by Zigzag, were distributed with some taste about the interior. Their native friends had shown their thoughtfulness by heaping a pile of dry sticks under the chimney, with more placed within reach. The starting of the fire was left to the lads. Nothing in the way of food was in sight, but the brothers had no fear of being forgotten or overlooked. It was several hours before nightfall, and they reclined on the furs to rest themselves before going outside. A dozen or more curious men and boys were lounging near, for the murmur of their voices reached the brothers, but no one ventured to intrude upon their privacy.

"George, when we get back to Ohio we shall be able to tell a story that will beat anything Simon Kenton can relate."

"How? There are not many that have passed through as much as he."

"But he has never been west of the Mississippi, and it isn't likely he ever will go. We must have gone two thousand miles beyond. When we see him again won't we make him open his eyes with our story of a winter among a tribe of Indians far over toward the Stony Mountains?"

"It will be a great story, indeed; but Victor, how are we going to pass the more than a hundred days that we must stay in this settlement?"

"Time goes fast enough when we are on the move, either shooting rapids in a river, riding our horses or tramping on foot, but it is mighty dull to sit still and do nothing, and we mustn't think of any such thing."

"But what shall we do?"

"What shall we do? Lots of things. We can hunt and fish, play games with the youngsters, learn to tramp on snowshoes when winter is fairly here, and, if Taggarak goes off on any raids, we ought to be able to make a full man apiece."

George looked into the face of his brother to see if he was in earnest.

"Do you mean that, Victor?"

"I certainly do. Why not?"

"It is well enough to fight when you have to, but Deerfoot will never let you do anything of that kind, nor would I agree to it. It would be trying to kill other people just for the fun of doing so, and *that* is contrary to what the Shawanoe has taught us."

"I suppose we shall have to get on as best we can with the other amusements, but I tremble when I think of the weather that will be here in a few weeks."

George looked around at the brown shaggy walls of buffalo fur. He grasped some of the long soft hairs in his palm and stroked the cool mass.

"We need never run short of fuel, and when the fire is going and the door shut I don't see why we shall not be as warm as in our own home at Woodvale. But what shall we *do*? *That's* the question. It will be tiresome beyond bearing to lie here stretched hour after hour during the day."

"Plague take it!" impatiently exclaimed Victor; "who is going to do anything of the kind? I should like to see Deerfoot let you sleep and lounge your days away. He will share the lodge with us, and you may be sure he'll keep things moving. There isn't any weather cold enough nor snow deep enough to hold him within doors, and he'll hustle you out with him. So let's hear no more of that. Then you mustn't forget, George, that we shall make lots of acquaintances among these people. We have learned to speak a good many words of Blackfoot, and shall learn more; we shall take a liking to some of these folks, and, if we have any kind of tact, shall make them like us. Most of them have never before looked upon a white person, but they will soon get over their wonder, and we shall all stand on the same level."

"Well, Victor, you have done a good deal to cheer me up. I guess it was the homesickness, after all, that made me blue. See here, these two fellows that put up this house for us have been such good friends that we must be able to call them by name."

"Mul-tal-la has repeated them several times to us."

"Now, will you repeat either of the names to me?"

"I couldn't do it to save my life. They are so long and outlandish that I can never get my, tongue around them."

"Let's give them shorter names."

"Well, suppose you name the taller one, who has such a crooked nose."

George reflected a moment and replied;

"I'll call him 'Spink;' that is short and easily remembered. I don't think he will be offended, for he seems to be good-natured."

"We can fancy that it may mean in some language, 'He that looks Sweeter than Honey,' and he will be delighted when we manage to make it clear with the help of Mul-tal-la. I have the other fellow named."

"What is it?"

"Jiggers, or, The Warrior that showed Chief Taggarak all He Knows. *That* ought to make him proud and happy."

So the two Blackfeet who had befriended the brothers received their names, and will be hereafter thus known when we refer to them, instead of using the difficult titles by which they were called by those of their own race.

From his seat opposite the door that was closed Victor had noticed a peculiar agitation now and then of the buffalo flap. Once, when the corner was drawn a little aside, he caught the sparkle of a bright eye, which was instantly withdrawn, as if the owner had noticed that his peeping was observed and he was scared. By and by the eye appeared again, and remained longer than before.

Victor smiled and crooked his finger at the peeping Tom. A moment later the flap was pulled aside, so as to display the head of an urchin some ten or twelve years old. Victor had whispered an explanation to his brother, and both looked at the boy, who had mustered up enough courage to step inside the tepee and then paused, as if afraid to come forward.

This young Blackfoot had the broadest, chubbiest face the boys had ever seen, and the grin on it seemed to touch each ear. He was short, stocky, and the picture of good nature. He wore no cap, and his thick black hair was cut so that it hung no lower than his chin on each side. He wore a hunting shirt, leggings and moccasins that were not very tidy, and he carried nothing in the nature of a weapon about him.

Victor and George could not restrain a laugh at the chap's appearance. The former continued to beckon to him, and said:

"Come here, Smiler, and shake hands with your friend."

He still hesitated, and, rising to his feet, Victor walked toward him, speaking so soothingly that the visitor kept his place, though apparently ready to duck his head and dash outdoors. He knew nothing about the ceremony of shaking hands, but he allowed Victor to take his palm in his own, and to lead him back to a seat on the furs between the brothers. A few minutes sufficed to make him feel at ease.

George and Victor called all their knowledge of Blackfoot into use, but they could not think of a word that was intelligible to the youngster, nor could they induce him to speak. He held his forefinger between his lips, shook his head now and then, and glanced slyly from one boy to the other, evidently well pleased but still embarrassed and a little distrustful.

Victor suddenly crossed over to where most of the contents of the pack carried by Zigzag had been laid out. Among these were several gaudy trinkets brought all the way from Woodvale and carefully reserved for special use. From the lot he took a string of bright crimson, blue and green beads, strung upon a linen thread, the loop being long enough to slip over the black crown and leave the lower part resting in all its dazzling beauty on the breast of the lad.

You cannot imagine the wonder and delight of the dusky urchin. For a few seconds he seemed too overcome to speak, and hardly breathed. He looked down at the glittering string, then drew his forefinger from between his lips and gingerly caressed the prize. Growing bolder, he raised the loop to his mouth as if to taste it. Pressing one of the beads with his even white teeth, the tiny glass snapped into fragments, some of which flew several feet away. The youngster was startled and glanced up at Victor, as if expecting a reproof.

The lad pleasantly shook his head to signify that the present did not form a staple article of food, and then the urchin slipped off the pile of furs and stood upon his sturdy legs. Looking gratefully up at the paleface he lifted the string over his head and handed the beads back to Victor. The latter took them from his hand and immediately slipped them about his neck again, thus showing that they belonged to the caller. Then the little one broke into grateful laughter, ran to the door, thrust aside the flap, and was gone.

"You couldn't have hit upon a better name than 'Smiler,'" said George Shelton, much amused by the peculiar visit they had received.

"Did you ever see one with so broad a grin? My only fear is that the other chaps will be jealous of him and expect us to give them presents, too. We haven't enough to go a tenth of the way round; but I couldn't refuse that codger."

The caller had not been gone two minutes when Mul-tal-la came in, bringing with him some buffalo meat that he had procured from a neighbor. It was uncooked, which was a small matter to the brothers, who were glad to see him, for he was the one person in the village with whom they could converse freely. Carefully placing the meat on several sticks, so as to protect it from dirt, he sat down to chat a few minutes with his young friends.

He told them of his visit to his father and mother, whose hearts were made as glad as his own, after their long separation; of his call on the father and mother of the companion whose body lay at rest many hundreds of miles away in the East, and of the comforting assurance that was now his that nothing was to be feared from the resentment of Chief Taggarak. Spink and Jiggers had received within the preceding ten days the assurance from the sachem himself, so that all uneasiness was gone from the heart of Mul-tal-la. But, had not the counsel of the two messengers been followed, nothing would have restrained Taggarak from taking the life of the one that had failed to bring back his comrade.

Victor told of the visit just received from the urchin, and of the present made to him, much to the lad's delight.

"We christened him 'Smiler,'" said Victor, "for I never saw such a grin on the face of man or boy."

"We could not help giving him the beads, but fear it will make trouble, for all the other boys in the village will want something, and we haven't supply for half a dozen."

"It might have been as my brothers say," replied Mul-tal-la, "if the boy had been the son of one of the ordinary warriors like myself, but he is not."

"Has he a distinguished father?" asked the wondering George.

"He is the son of Taggarak, our great war chief."

"I never dreamed of that," exclaimed the pleased Victor. "It surely could not have happened better. How is it that he was braver than the other boys and came into the lodge when all the others kept at a distance?"

"That," said the Blackfoot significantly, "is because he is the son of Taggarak and *knows it*. He can do nothing that can bring him punishment, unless it comes from his father, and he does not punish him unless he acts as if he is afraid of something."

"How many children has Taggarak?"

"Only two—the one whom you saw, who bears the same name as his father, and another boy about half as old, who is Ap-pa-pa-alk. He promises to grow up like his father and to become one of the greatest warriors among all the Blackfeet."

"When the chief learns that Taggarak Junior and we have become friends, and he sees the beads around the neck of his boy, will he not be pleased and feel kindly toward us, who gave him the little present?"

Mul-tal-la was thoughtful for a minute before replying.

"The war chief is a man of strange moods. It may make no difference in his feelings toward my brothers, but Mul-tal-la does not think he will *hate* them for what they have done."

CHAPTER XIII.
SUMMONED TO COURT.

At the end of a week George and Victor Shelton had become full-fledged Blackfoot citizens. Several causes united to bring about this pleasant state of affairs. In the first place, the boys used tact and good sense. If the attention they drew to themselves became annoying at times they did not allow their new friends to see it. They played with the dusky youths, and were not sorry to find plenty no older than they who could outrun and outjump them. It was too cold to go in swimming, but one day when George and Victor were crossing the stream in front of the village with three other lads, one of whom was their young friend

Smiler, heir apparent to the Blackfoot throne, the overloaded canoe suddenly sank below its gunwales, and all had to swim through the icy waters to shore. Every one of the three arrived first, and Smiler beat them all, though in this instance I cannot help suspecting that the two young Blackfeet favored the prince, but they beat the brothers fairly.

When the weather was good there were sometimes as many as fifty lads playing on the common or cleared space at the rear of the village. They indulged in a species of foot-ball, like the modern game, which was marked by the roughest kind of play. In violence it sometimes approached our own foot-ball, and blows were often given and received in the fierce rushing.

On a certain forenoon, in a particularly exciting contest, one of the players landed a blow on the side of Victor's head, which sent him sprawling to earth. His quick temper flashed into a flame, and he leaped up with doubled fists and made for the offender, who coolly awaited him. A warning cry from George recalled his brother to his senses, and, instead of attacking his assailant, he laughingly plunged into the melee, which went on as merrily as before.

When five Indian youths invited their guests to go on a hunt the boys took their rifles, but their hosts carried only bows and arrows. On the return of the tired party at nightfall they brought the choice portions of three antelopes, two of which were slain by the youthful Blackfeet, while the one that George Shelton had brought down received also an effective thrust from an arrow. The dusky hunters "guyed" the palefaces who could not do as well as they with their primitive weapons, even though the fire spouted from the iron tubes and the balls that could not be seen by the eye carried death farther than did the missiles launched by the natives. George and Victor took it all in good part, and did not resent the taunts that were numerous.

Another strong contributing cause to the popularity of the Shelton boys was Mul-tal-la, He was home but a short time when everyone in the village knew of the generous hospitality he had received from the boys and their friends. This appeal to the gratitude of the Blackfeet produced the best effect. Mul-tal-la and the messengers, Spink and Jiggers, had something to add, and their stories of the remarkable young Shawanoe roused much curiosity to see him and witness some of the exploits of which he was said to be capable.

Chief Taggarak did not return until nearly a week after the arrival of the brothers, and then he kept much to himself. He was reserved and gloomy, and though George and Victor caught several glimpses of him, and though they continued to make much of his two boys, for the younger moved about the settlement as freely as the elder, the great war chief ignored the presence of the visitors until he had been at home for several days.

One afternoon, after the return of a party from a hunt, Mul-tal-la appeared at the lodge of George and Victor with word that the chief wished them to come before him for a talk. The boys knew so little of the Blackfoot tongue that Mul-tal-la was to act as interpreter.

"What does he wish with us?" asked George, who, like Victor, felt some misgiving as to the object of this command.

"Mul-tal-la does not know, but his brothers need have no fear."

"What did he say to you?" asked Victor.

"Only that he wished to see and talk with you. Come with me."

It was about the middle of the afternoon when the lads, under the lead of their dusky friend, threaded their way among the tepees to one near the middle of the village, which might be considered the royal residence. This structure differed from the others in that it was double the capacity of an ordinary lodge, that one side consisted of a broad face of rock, that it was in the shape of a square, supported at two corners by upright poles, the rock serving as the remaining support. The fire was always kindled against the base of this mass of stone, an opening just above serving as an outlet for the smoke.

When the visitors arrived Taggarak was alone, seated at one side of the large apartment, with a small fire burning in its usual place. His royal consort and two children were excluded from the conference.

The war chief was about forty years of age, and his face showed him to be a man of exceptional ability and mental strength. It was easy to understand the iron will with which he ruled the turbulent and warlike Blackfeet. He had thrown aside his blanket and sat in a close-fitting shirt of deerskin, with girdle at the waist, and with leggings and moccasins.

Taggarak was not a handsome Indian, but he was of striking mien. His long black hair, without ornament of any kind, dangled about his shoulders; his mouth was broad; his nose well formed; his eyes black and piercing, rather small, and seemed to glitter with fire from under his eyebrows. His cheek-bones were prominent, the chin square and firm, and the expression of the countenance stern to the last degree. Wrinkles already showed in his low, wide forehead and at the corners of his eyes. There were two scars on one cheek, and his arms and body, had they been uncovered, would have revealed many more, for Taggarak was a mighty warrior, who had beaten down many foes in single combat, and had eagerly risked his life in resisting the desperate raids made against his tribe, or in pushing invasions among others of his own race. Unlike many of his own people, he never was vain enough to wear the scalp-lock, nor did he disfigure his face with paint. When he went upon the warpath his enemies speedily found it out, without any such childish notices.

Mul-tal-la led the way into the imperial wigwam, the brothers closely following. The three respectfully saluted the chief, who looked keenly at them as they entered, and, without returning their greeting, pointed to a pile of furs on the farther side of the lodge, where the callers seated themselves, removed their caps, and awaited the pleasure of the great man.

An Ominous Interview.

You will be better pleased with a free translation of the conversation, remembering that Mul-tal-la acted as the mouthpiece of the chief and the boys, though the latter had picked up enough knowledge of the tongue to catch the meaning of a good many of the words spoken by Taggarak, who, of course, knew nothing of English.

"My sons have come a long way from the land of the rising sun. Why did they leave their friends to make so long a journey?"

"We loved Mul-tal-la, and wished to look upon the great and good chieftain Taggarak, of whom Mul-tal-la said many words of praise."

This reply was made by Victor, and was duly filtrated through the interpreter, who was pleased with the words so flattering to himself. It must be admitted that when Victor tried his hand he showed himself a promising student of diplomacy.

George thought it well to add his answer:

"Hunters told us of the great land that lay toward the setting sun, and we longed to look upon it, as Mul-tal-la and his friend longed to look upon the country where we make our home."

"When do my sons go back to their dwelling place?"

"The snows will be deep in the mountains for many moons; the palefaces will perish if they try to labor through them. They will wait till the sun melts the snows, and the buds come on the trees and the singing of the birds trembles in the air. They will be glad to do this if the great Taggarak is not displeased to have them stay among his people."

This had the sound of a hint for an invitation. Being such, however, it failed of its purpose, for the chieftain ignored it. Perhaps he did not think it worth the trouble to tell the youths they were welcome; that was to be assumed from the hospitality already shown them.

"Taggarak has heard of a wonderful warrior who came from the land of the rising sun. Where is he?"

"He has a horse that he loved, which was lost, and he is searching for him."

"There are many horses among the Blackfeet; he could have one of them."

"But there is none like the black stallion of Deerfoot."

"Where did the warrior get him!"

"The stallion was the leader of a drove of wild horses. Deerfoot sought him out and conquered him without saddle or bridle or the help of anyone."

This statement seemed so incredible that Mul-tal-la felt it necessary to add his own statement that the words of the pale-faced lad were true, for he had seen the exploit of the Shawanoe with his own eyes. Even then it is to be feared the chieftain refused to believe the story.

"Are all the Shawanoes like this warrior!"

"There is none like him," was the reply of Victor Shelton, whose full answer was faithfully translated to Chief Taggarak. "The Shawanoes, nor Wyandots, nor Chippewas, nor Nez Perces, nor Shoshones, nor Assiniboines, nor any tribe are as great as the Blackfeet. Had Deerfoot been a member of any of them, he would have been the greatest among them all, with the exception of the mighty Taggarak, whom no one can equal."

Ah, but this youth from the Buckeye State was sly. He looked at the rigid coppery countenance of the chieftain as these words were interpreted to him. The youth thought he detected a sparkle of the small black eyes, but I fear it was only fancy.

"Why is he called Deerfoot?"

"The palefaces gave him that name because no deer can run as fast as he."

"My sons speak with a double tongue," said the chief, frowning.

"They might in the presence of anyone but Taggarak, but to him they use only a single tongue. Let the great chieftain wait and see Deerfoot for himself."

Unquestionably Victor was advancing fast along the path of diplomacy.

"When will the Shawanoe be with the Blackfeet, who wait to welcome him?"

"We hope not many suns will set before he comes; but he has had a long way to journey, and may have to slay other warriors that are not willing to let Deerfoot have his steed."

"The Shawanoe may fall and never see his paleface brothers again."

"We have no fear of that," airily replied George. The next question of Taggarak was as startling as unexpected:

"Does the Shawanoe teach the religion of the red men or that of the palefaces?"

The brothers looked significantly at each other as Mul-tal-la translated these words, but Victor scarcely hesitated in his reply.

"Deerfoot teaches the religion that he believes is true. It is of a Great Spirit, who wishes his children to live in friendship with one another; not to make war; to show mercy to all; to be forgiving and do what they can to make other people happy. Such is the wish of the Great Spirit. Deerfoot lives according to that faith, and we believe in it, and try to do as he does."

The chief looked steadily in the face of the youth while he was speaking, though he did not understand a syllable until it was properly rendered by Mul-tal-la. Victor gazed as unflinchingly into the fierce countenance before him, while uttering the noble sentiments. His self-respect forbade any shrinking on his part when such a question was put to him. As the interpreter waited for him to finish, Victor added:

"Tell him exactly what I said."

"And that the answer is from both of us," added George.

Mul-tal-la obeyed, but carefully refrained from saying that he, too, had accepted the new religion, and that the warriors who acted as messengers were pondering over it, and had spoken to some of their comrades on the momentous theme. It is not for us to censure the red man if he was cautious, for, if need be, he was ready to die for the truth.

The thin lips of Taggarak curled with scorn when he caught the full meaning of the reply of the youth. His patience was gone.

"The Shawanoe does not belong to the tribe of Taggarak. My sons, the palefaces, are of another race; they may believe any lies they choose, for it is naught to Taggarak. But none of Taggarak's people shall believe it! And if the Shawanoe seeks to turn them from the faith of their fathers, the Shawanoe shall die! My sons will tell the Shawanoe what Taggarak has said, that when he comes among the Blackfeet he shall live. Taggarak has spoken, and my sons may go. They will not forget the words of Taggarak."

CHAPTER XIV.
A NEW BLACKFOOT CITIZEN.

The words of Taggarak the war chief weighed heavily upon George and Victor Shelton, for nothing was more certain to them than that trouble for Deerfoot was near. He could not be frightened into any attempt to hide his light under a bushel, or to deny the faith that was woven into the very fibre of his being. The brothers talked the question over many times. It was never referred to between them and Mul-tal-la, for the Blackfoot could give them no help, and the final solution of the problem must be reached by Deerfoot himself.

Our young friends joined as earnestly in the games, the fishing and hunting as ever, and no one looking upon them would have dreamed that they suffered any discomfort of mind. Thus the days passed until two more weeks had gone by, and they began to wonder at the long absence of the Shawanoe.

There had been a flurry of snow, and the weather was perceptibly colder. As they sat in their lodge after finishing their late meal, the sifting of the needle-like points against the bison hides was soothing to the ear, and the crackling wood fire gave a cheerful illumination to the interior.

Reclining on the soft warm robes, they recurred to the theme that was continually in their thoughts.

"I am almost sorry we ever came to this place," said George, with a sigh. "We have had an interesting experience, have made a number of friends, such as they are, though there can never be much in the way of friendship between us and these people."

"How could we have spent the winter, which will be cold and severe?" asked his brother.

"Deerfoot would have had no trouble in finding some cave in the rocks which we could have fitted up into as good a house as this. There are places, too, where the horses would have been sheltered from the storms, and we could gather plenty of cottonwood bark when grass was beyond reach, and thus kept the animals alive."

"Perhaps that might have been done, but I don't believe it is as easy as you think. It seems to me our hope is in Deerfoot's tact. He will not listen in silence to any attack upon his faith, and when the heathen inquire of him he will answer them truly, but he has enough respect for the rank of Taggarak not to offend him when there is no need of doing so."

"You see he has already sown seed, and there will be inquiries by others from him. Spink and Jiggers have been thoughtful a long time. They have spoken to others. Mul-tal-la must have done the same, though he is cautious and fears to offend the chief. All these and many others will question Deerfoot, who will answer them without thought or care, even though a hundred Taggaraks stood in his way."

"Tact is a good thing, but all that I can see it is likely to do in this case is to postpone the trouble."

In the midst of their gloomy talk, and with the snow still rattling against the dry bison robes of their tepee, the flap was suddenly lifted and Deerfoot the Shawanoe entered and caught the hand of each delighted boy. His face was aglow with health and pleasure, for they were no happier than he over the reunion.

They slapped him on the shoulder, shook his hand again and again, and plied him with so many questions that minutes passed before there was anything like coherence in their boisterous chatter.

"Where did you leave Whirlwind?" asked George, thereby implying that he had not a shadow of doubt of the success of the venture of the young Shawanoe.

"This afternoon, when coming from the east to this settlement," replied their friend, "Deerfoot came in sight of Mul-tal-la, who was hunting alone. He had just shot an antelope, and we sat down and ate it together. Then we came to the village as it was growing dark. Mul-tal-la showed Deerfoot where the horses are free. There is snow on the ground, but not enough to hide all the grass, and Deerfoot was told of a place to the west, where Mul-tal-la says the shelter sometimes permits the grass to keep green all winter. There the horses will soon be taken, and shelter has been made for them. Whirlwind, after Deerfoot had talked with him, consented to go among the horses, as Zigzag, Prince and the others have done. He does not like to mingle with common animals, and is as proud as ever."

"We have enough left of our buffalo meat to furnish you a meal, Deerfoot, but you told us you had eaten only a little while ago."

"Deerfoot thanks his brothers, and will not eat until to-morrow."

"I suppose Mul-tal-la told you all about us?"

"He has left little for you to tell. Deerfoot is glad to hear his brothers have been so well, but they have much to say that he would like to hear."

"O Deerfoot!" exclaimed Victor; "tell us how you got Whirlwind back. You must have had a pretty hard time, for you were gone a month."

The three seated themselves on the soft furs, George first throwing additional wood on the blaze, and the Shawanoe, knowing how interested his friends were, modestly related the story with which you became familiar long ago. The boys were so absorbed in the narration that they did not speak nor move until it was ended. He made light of the dangers and difficulties which he overcame, and it was plain to his listeners that he slurred over more than one of his most remarkable exploits.

The brothers found it almost amusing to hear that the young Shawanoe had so wrenched one of his ankles that he could not use it for a time. It was so remarkable to learn that he had suffered from anything of that nature that they found it hard to associate the two. The manner in which Deerfoot stepped into the tent proved that he did not feel the slightest effects of the hurt. The Shawanoe told his friends that he and Mul-tal-la had purposely tarried outside the village until dark, because the newcomer did not care to have his arrival become known until the morrow. He wished to enjoy the first evening undisturbed with his old friends. Being on foot, with a blanket about his shoulders like Mul-tal-la and many other Blackfeet, he looked so much like one of them in the night that he attracted no notice, and Mul-tal-la promised to tell no one of the presence of the youth whom all were eager to see.

It was not until late in the evening that the Shawanoe spoke of the theme that had troubled the brothers so long. Mul-tal-la had told him of the conversation with Taggarak, and he asked the boys to give their recollection, not omitting a word they could recall. Their friend listened gravely, and was silent when they had finished, his dark eyes fixed upon the fire in the middle of the lodge, as if his meditations had drifted beyond the time and place. After waiting for several minutes, Victor said:

"Deerfoot, you can't know how much we are worried. We understand how you feel and that no danger can scare you into denying the true religion, any more than it can scare George and me, but you may as well be careful and avoid rousing the anger of Taggarak, so long as there is no need of provoking him."

"What would my brothers have Deerfoot do?" gently asked, the Shawanoe.

"We don't know," replied George. "Vic and I have talked about this a hundred times since our call on the chief, and we are puzzled as well as worried."

"Are my brothers ready to die for the religion?"

"We are, and will prove it if it ever becomes necessary; but," added Victor, "we don't see the need of dying when there isn't any need of it."

This original bit of philosophy caused Deerfoot to turn and look with a half-serious expression into the face of Victor.

"How great is the wisdom of my brother! Who taught him such things?"

Then assuming a graver countenance, but gazing steadily at his friend, he added:

"There was One who died on the cross for you and Deerfoot."

There was a world of meaning in these words, and they fitly closed the conversation for the night. All lay down soon after and slept until morning.

The snow ceased falling, and only a thin coating lay on the ground at daylight. An unusual moderation in the temperature carried this away before nightfall, and the weather became almost spring-like, or rather resembled the lingering days of Indian summer, which are the expiring gasp of the mild season, soon to be followed by the biting rigors of winter.

Before noon it was known throughout the Blackfoot village that the remarkable young Shawanoe had arrived. The excitement was greater than that caused by the coming of Victor and George Shelton, and for a time Deerfoot was seriously annoyed, but he strove to bear it with the sensible philosophy of his nature. Those who saw him as he moved here and there with the boys, or Mul-tal-la, or Spink and Jiggers, had to admit the truth of the assertion heard many times; he was the most prepossessing young warrior upon whom any of them had ever looked. Neither among the Blackfeet nor any of their neighboring tribes had so comely a youth been seen. And this being the fact, many were more unwilling than before to believe he was so powerful, so active, so fleet of foot and so athletic as had been claimed. This doubt was not lessened by the conduct of Deerfoot himself. He soon became acquainted with nearly everyone in the village, and went upon hunting expeditions with them, but displayed no more skill than most of his companions. He avoided all trials of speed, though often invited to take part by the doubters. In crossing the river in a canoe with two of his new acquaintances, he swung a paddle, while each of them did the same. The Blackfeet saw no evidence of skill superior to theirs, because in truth none was displayed. He was urged to take part in their games, but made excuse to act only as spectator. He did not wish to become a competitor and deceive the others by not doing his best. His modesty led him to shrink from exhibiting his abilities. Moreover, he had a feeling that it savored of ingratitude or lack of appreciation of the hospitality he was receiving to place himself at the fore, as he knew he could readily do.

But it had to come. Too many boasts had been made by the friends of Deerfoot for the envious Blackfeet to allow the Shawanoe to rest upon such laurels. Neither Mul-tal-la nor the brothers would abate one bit of their claims. Deerfoot would have stopped them had not the mischief, as he viewed it, been done before his coming. He could only remain mute and hope the matter would die out of itself. But that was impossible.

The most noted test of athletic skill that ever occurred in the history of the Blackfeet tribe took place one bright, keen, sunshiny afternoon on the bleak plain at the rear of the village. A week had been spent in making the preparations as thorough as they could be made. Runners came from three of the other villages, and they were the flower of the tribe—lithe, sinewy, swift and splendid specimens of manly beauty, symmetry and grace. Each was worthy of being called a champion, and all were confident of lowering the colors of the dusky stranger from the land of the rising sun, who had been presumptuous enough to be persuaded to enter a trial that must disgrace him. More than one believed that in his chagrin the Shawanoe would hasten from the village and never more be seen in that part of the world.

Now, it would be interesting to tell all about this memorable tournament, but you have no more doubt of the result than did the victor from the moment he consented to enter into it. Mul-tal-la and the Shelton brothers, including Spink and Jiggers, impressed upon the Shawanoe the necessity of his doing his best, no matter what the nature of the struggle might be. He promised to follow their counsel, as he did that of Simon Kenton at the foot race at Woodvale the year before.

Five contestants entered against Deerfoot. The distance was about two hundred yards. Never before was the Shawanoe pitted against such fleet runners, but he finished the struggle fifty feet in front of the foremost. The spectators, as well as the defeated runners themselves, were dazed, and could hardly credit their own senses.

Not less crushing were Deerfoot's victories in the running, the standing and the high jump. Like all great athletes, his triumphs seemed to be won without calling upon his reserve capacity, and therefore with much less apparent effort than shown by his rivals. In firing at a target, he left the few marksmen of the tribe hopelessly out of sight. Then he borrowed Mul-tal-la's bow, and every arrow that he launched went farther and truer than any other. Altogether it was a great day for Deerfoot the Shawanoe.

CHAPTER XV.
THE SPIRIT CIRCLE.

Never in all their lives were the Shelton brothers prouder of Deerfoot the Shawanoe than when they saw him utterly defeat the finest athletes of the Blackfoot tribe. The youth had done his best, as he was urged to do, and his triumph was too overwhelming for anyone to question it. He had been pitted against the very flower of that powerful people, who at that time numbered between three and four thousand souls. The pick of the runners and marksmen had come from the other villages, and every one was decisively vanquished.

The delight of Mul-tal-la and of Spink and Jiggers was hardly less than that of the boys. Mul-tal-la *knew* the Shawanoe would win, while the other two Blackfeet merely believed it, for they had never been intimately associated with the champion of champions, and only remembered what Mul-tal-la told them he had witnessed.

Human nature is the same the world over, and among the defeated ones was a feeling of envy and resentment toward the young warrior who belonged to another tribe, and who, after coming many hundreds of miles, had put them all to shame. This was to be expected, and it caused no uneasiness to Deerfoot, who had faced it many times among his own race as well as on the part of white people.

But the Shawanoe took little or no pleasure in his victory. He had entered into the contest because he could not help it. Had he reached the village at the same time with his friends, he would have sternly forbidden any reference to his brilliant physical powers, and thus prevented the tournament that was so distasteful to him; but, as I have shown, the mischief was done before he came upon the scene. His reputation had been proclaimed, and naught remained but to prove that only the simple truth had been told of him.

That evening the four friends who had spent so many days and nights together were gathered in the lodge at the northern end of the village. Time had been given for the excitement to die out. Three of the defeated champions were well on their way to their own village, when, had the result been different, they would have staid for several days in what may be considered the Blackfoot capital. The hum and murmur of voices and the restless moving to and fro were audible outside, but the old companions were left to themselves. Mul-tal-la had succeeded in impressing upon his countrymen that when their guests retired to their tepee they were not to be intruded upon.

The fire was burning in the middle of the primitive home, and George and Victor Shelton and Mul-tal-la were seated on the furs that were spread along three sides of the apartment. Deerfoot sat by himself, removed from all. He was partly reclining on one elbow and gazing into the fire, as if sunk in meditation. The boys knew the meaning of his attitude and air; he was dissatisfied with what had occurred that day.

"By gracious!" said Victor; "if I could do what you did, Deerfoot, I'd be so proud I wouldn't speak to George or Mul-tal-la or you; and yet you don't seem to feel a bit stuck up. You ought to be ashamed of yourself."

The Shawanoe made no reply, but continued gazing into the fire, as if he did not hear the words. George added:

"Your victory will be talked about among all the Blackfoot villages, and the children of to-day will tell their children about it long after we are gone."

Mul-tal-la kept glancing at Deerfoot with an admiring, affectionate expression, and, noting his continued silence, he said in a gentle voice:

"The Blackfeet did not think Mul-tal-la spoke with a single tongue; they said his words were lies, but they do not say so now."

"I didn't see anything of Taggarak," added Victor. "I looked around for him after the battle was won. Why did he stay away?"

Deerfoot for the first time noted what was said. He lifted his head from his elbow and sat upright.

"Taggarak was there; Deerfoot saw him," he quietly remarked.

"Yes; Mul-tal-la passed near him. The chief kept by himself and spoke to no one. He was on the side nearest the wood. Just before the last race was won he turned away and went back to his lodge."

"What was the meaning of *that*?" asked the Shawanoe. "Is he displeased with the defeat of his young men?"

"It is the other way; he is glad their conceit has been checked. The Blackfeet are great boasters, and he has reproved them many times. Mul-tal-la saw him smile when Deerfoot came home many paces in front of that tall warrior, who is the greatest boaster of them all. Taggarak was glad when he was defeated."

"It pleases us more than we can tell to know that Deerfoot has won the good-will of the war chief," observed George Shelton, who could not forget that ominous conversation they had had some time before with Taggarak. "It will make our stay more pleasant than I believed it would be."

The observant Victor noticed that Mul-tal-la gave no reply to this remark, which had been made in the hope of being confirmed by the Blackfoot. The latter glanced at the Shawanoe, whose eyes again rested upon the fire. George threw a couple of sticks in the blaze and then resumed his seat beside his brother. When the stillness was becoming oppressive, Mul-tal-la startled all three of his listeners by what was certainly a remarkable question:

"Is Deerfoot afraid of any man?"

Even the Shawanoe flashed a surprised look upon the Blackfoot.

"Why does my brother ask Deerfoot that?"

"He shall soon know. Will Deerfoot answer Mul-tal-la?"

The question seemed to rouse the Shawanoe, who spoke with more animation than he had shown since the group had come together for the evening.

"No; Deerfoot fears no man that lives! God has given him more power and skill than he deserves. He has never denied protection to Deerfoot. He has told him to do right, and Deerfoot tries to obey His will. When He thinks the time has come for Deerfoot to go to Him, Deerfoot will be ready and will be glad. Deerfoot knows He is not pleased with such things as took place to-day. What is it for one man to run faster or shoot straighter than another? No credit belongs to *him*, for it is God who gives him the power. Deerfoot would sin if he shrank from any task laid upon him; but a victory like that just won does no one any good. Deerfoot would be happier if he could turn the thoughts of all those people to the true God."

In the warmth of his feelings the Shawanoe had wandered from the question just asked him, but in doing so he revealed the nobility of his nature. He was oppressed by the belief that the strife in which he had been the victor not only accomplished no real good, but actually retarded the work he had in mind. He came back to the question his friend had just asked.

"Why does my brother think Deerfoot is afraid of any man?"

Mul-tal-la could not hide a certain nervousness, but with all the calmness he could summon he parried the direct question by the remark:

"The most terrible warrior of all the Blackfeet is Taggarak the chieftain; he has slain many men in battle and has never been conquered."

The inference from this remark was obvious even to the boys. It was Victor who asked in surprise:

"Is Deerfoot to fight with Taggarak? If he does, I'll bet on Deerfoot."

To any others except those present the words of the Shawanoe would have sounded like boasting, but there was no such thought in his heart.

"Deerfoot has no more fear of Taggarak than he has of a pappoose. He may be a great warrior, but Deerfoot has conquered as great warriors as he."

Determined that Mul-tal-la should parry no longer, the Shawanoe forced him to a direct answer.

"Why does my brother think Taggarak wishes to fight him?"

The reply was astonishing:

"The squaw of Taggarak is seeking to learn of the God that she has been told is known to the Shawanoe. She has asked me, she has asked Kepkapkolakak and Borabtrik (the messengers known as 'Spink' and 'Jiggers'). She does not sleep because of her heaviness of mind."

"Does Taggarak know of this?" asked the surprised Deerfoot.

"Not yet; but it must soon come to his knowledge."

"Will he harm his wife?"

"Mul-tal-la cannot say; he may put her to death. There is no doubt that he will slay Deerfoot—*if he can*," added the Blackfoot significantly, "or he will make him walk around the Spirit Circle till he drops dead."

Deerfoot stared in astonishment. He was mystified.

"The Spirit Circle," he repeated. "Does Deerfoot hear aright? If so, what does his brother mean? Deerfoot is listening."

Thus appealed to, the Blackfoot was silent for a minute, as if gathering his thoughts. He looked up at the opening in the roof of the lodge, then into the fire, and, addressing the three, repeated the following myth or legend, which has been extant among the Blackfeet Indians from time immemorial:

"Many, many moons ago, long before the parents of our oldest men were born, a chieftain as great as Taggarak ruled the Blackfeet. His fame reached far to the north, to the east, to the south and to the west, beyond the Stony Mountains, to the shore of the great water, for there was none like him. In those far-away days the home of Wahla, chieftain of the Blackfeet, was to the south of this village, on the banks of the Two Rivers.

"Wahla had a daughter who was the most beauteous maiden that warrior ever looked upon. She was loving and dainty, and the idol of the stern old warrior, who would have cut off his right hand rather than have the slightest harm come to her. Never did father love daughter more than Chief Wahla loved Mita the Rose of the Forest.

"Wahla returned one day from a fierce battle with the Cheyennes. A great victory had been won, and the Blackfeet brought home a score of prisoners, that they might be tied to the stake and burned while their captives made merry over their sufferings. This was the custom of the Blackfeet, and they have not yet forgotten such amusements.

"Among the captives was a manly youth, who was proud and brave, and had slain three of the Blackfeet and wounded Wahla himself before they made him prisoner. He scorned to ask mercy, which would have been denied him, and, without a tremor of limb or a dimming of his bright eyes, awaited the cruel death that he knew had been prepared for him and his comrades.

"Wahla had to keep his captives for a week or more until word could be sent to the other villages, that they might come and feast upon the deaths of the Cheyennes. During that time, Mul-tal-la cannot tell how, the young Cheyenne warrior and Mita, daughter of the chieftain, met and learned to love each other. No one knew their secret, and so, while preparations were going on for the cruel deaths, she managed to loose his bonds, and one night the two fled for the home of the Cheyennes, there to become husband and wife.

"Wahla did not learn of the flight of his daughter and lover until the next morning, when he started in pursuit. He went alone, for his rage was so terrible that he was not willing anyone should share the sweetness of revenge with him. He traveled fast, and drew nigh enough to catch sight of the two on the second day following their flight. He did not carry his bow, but had his knife and tomahawk, while the youth possessed no weapon at all. Had a knife been his, he would not have used it against Wahla, because he was the father of the maiden whom he loved more than his life.

"When the two found they could not flee faster than the wrathful chieftain, they paused and waited for him to come up. Then Mita threw herself at the feet of her father and prayed him to spare the life of the Cheyenne. The chief spurned her and ran after the young warrior. The youth did not flee, but stood with folded arms, calmly awaiting him.

"'Slay me,' he said, 'but when I die Mita will die with me!'

"Heedless of the appeal, the furious chieftain plunged his knife into the breast of the youth, who sank to the earth and breathed out his life. Wahla turned to seize his daughter, but at that moment a wild shriek rent the air, and she died, clasping his knees and moaning that he had slain her as well as the Cheyenne.

"When Wahla saw what he had done, he started to hurry to his village, but his mind had gone from him. You were told that he had been wounded by the Cheyenne in battle. The wound was in the thigh of the chief, and it now broke out afresh, as if in punishment for the crime he had committed. It made him limp sorely, but he would not stop, and ran faster than ever. Because of his halt gait, he ran in a circle.

"Round and round he went all night, when he perished, but the Great Spirit kept him running throughout the days and weeks that followed until he became a shadow. His feet wore a circular path, which may be seen to-day, as Mul-tal-la has looked upon it many times and my brothers may do if they will journey a few days to the southward.

"But Mul-tal-la now tells the strangest part of this story. In the years that have passed since Wahla slew the Cheyenne lover, and his daughter died at his feet, the storms would have wiped away all signs of the path long ago. But it remains as distinct as ever. This is because the spirit of Wahla tramps it round and round all through the nights when the moon does not shine, for no one can see him running over the ground.

"When you look toward the slope of the mountain you can see the circle as plain as we see those sticks burning in the middle of the lodge, but when you reach the spot no sign of the path shows."

"How is that?" asked the wondering Victor.

"It is the belief that the spirit of Mita, the daughter, is always hovering over the spot, and that her heart forever grieves for her father and lover. When she sees anyone drawing near the place, she hurries from her home, which is near at hand, though no one knows exactly where, and, bending over the ground, hurries along and flirts a piece of her garment over the whole length of the path and blots it out, so that grass grows where a few minutes before was only the hard earth, packed by the moccasins of her father."

"What brings the path into sight again?" asked George Shelton.

"When night comes, Chief Wahla begins tramping around the circle once more. At sunrise the path is as it was before, and so remains unless some one starts forward to gain a closer look. The moment he does so the invisible spirit of Mita, daughter of Wahla, hurries out and destroys all the footprints, so that no one has ever been near enough to gain a close view of them, nor can he ever do so. Such is the legend of the Spirit Circle."[1]

CHAPTER XVI.
THE FIELD OF HONOR.

Deerfoot did not interrupt the Blackfoot while he was relating the legend of the Spirit Circle. He listened attentively. He had heard many such myths among his own people, and once they impressed him, but he had come to look upon them as idle tales not worth a thought. Instead of commenting upon the rude beauty of the story that had been told to his friend many years before, he asked the practical question:

"What has the Spirit Circle to do with Deerfoot and Taggarak?"

"It is the law among the Blackfeet that when our war chief Taggarak wills to punish some great criminal he sends him to the Spirit Circle, where he must walk around it without food or drink till he drops down and dies."

"Has anyone ever done that?" asked the Shawanoe.

"Yes; more than once. Not many moons ago a warrior killed his father, mother and child in a fit of rage. The only punishment that fitted such an awful crime was that of the Spirit Circle. Three warriors took the man there and started him round the path; they took turns in watching, and made sure that he had no food nor water, and was kept moving till he could move no longer. He fell down, and they stood near until he breathed his last; then they came back to Taggarak and told him what had been done."

"My brother has not yet shown what his words have to do with Deerfoot and Taggarak."

"Let my brother have patience and he shall know. Deerfoot remembers the rock from whose top he first caught sight of Mul-tal-la, whose brother was coming to this village, riding on Whirlwind?"

As he spoke the Blackfoot pointed to the east. Deerfoot nodded. The meeting place was a half mile beyond the open space on which the athletic contests had been held that day.

"It is the command of Taggarak that the Shawanoe shall meet him there tomorrow, when the sun climbs the mountain tops. He must bring only his hunting knife and come alone; the chief will do the same. When they face each other, Taggarak will give the Shawanoe the choice of dying by his hand or at the Spirit Circle."

"Did Taggarak say *that* to my brother?"

"That is his command. He has heard that the Shawanoe is making squaws of his warriors; he therefore gives him his choice of deaths."

Victor Shelton sprang to his feet.

"See here, Mul-tal-la," he said, excitedly; "do you tell us that the chief Taggarak makes the condition that he and Deerfoot are each to use only his knife as a weapon?"

The Blackfoot gravely nodded his head.

"And that neither is to have a friend with him?"

"So Taggarak wills."

"That isn't the way people fight duels. George and I must be on hand when Deerfoot gets into a scrape like that."

"But it cannot be."

"My brothers will stay here till Deerfoot comes back to them," quietly remarked the Shawanoe.

"But how are we to know that Taggarak won't play some trick on us? He may have half a dozen of his warriors hiding among the bushes or rocks, so as to help him kill Deerfoot."

For the first time in the interview Mul-tal-la smiled.

"Taggarak never breaks his word. He might do as my brothers say if he thought there was need of it. He doesn't believe the Shawanoe will be more than a child in his hands when the two stand in front of each other."

"He might have thought that yesterday, or at any time before the games to-day, but after he saw Deerfoot perform he must have some doubt."

"Deerfoot did not fight. Taggarak knows naught of his skill in doing that, even though he has been told he killed a grizzly bear in a fair struggle. He would feel ashamed if he asked for any help against the Shawanoe."

Deerfoot calmly rose to his feet. Those who looked up at him noted a peculiar flash of his dark eyes that was not often seen, and, when seen, told of the hidden fires he was holding in subjection. He raised his hand for silence.

"Let Deerfoot speak. He knows where the rock is that Taggarak says shall be the meeting place between him and me. His command shall be obeyed. Deerfoot will be there, with only his knife to defend himself. He has said he does not fear the Blackfoot chieftain. Let my brothers speak of something else."

The boys and even Mul-tal-la were so full of the theme that it was hard for them to talk or think of anything beside. They would have questioned the Shawanoe as to his plans and intentions, but he would not permit. The hour was growing late, and the Blackfoot remained but a short time, when he bade all good-night and passed out of the tepee.

Respecting the mood of Deerfoot, neither Victor nor George made any further reference to the momentous morrow. They disrobed and stretched out on their soft couches, while the Shawanoe, taking his Bible from the bosom of his hunting shirt, reclined on one elbow—his favorite attitude at such times—so that the light fell on the printed page. He read in his low, musical voice until, suspecting the truth, he paused and looked across at the brothers. Both were asleep. He smiled, read awhile longer to himself and then joined them in the land of dreams, sinking into slumber as quickly as they, and within the ten minutes following his own prayer.

The morning dawned dull, chilly and clouded, with threats of snow in the air. The Shawanoe was the first to awake, and busied himself in his usual noiseless fashion with renewing the fire and preparing the morning meal from the antelope meat, of which enough was on hand to last for several meals. The salt and pepper brought by the boys from home had been used up long before, and they had accustomed themselves to get on without the condiments which seem so much of a necessity with us.

The breakfast was eaten with the usual deliberation, none of the three speaking of the event that was impending, though the brothers were full of it. When Deerfoot arose, drew his knife from his girdle, carefully inspected it and then shoved it back in place and glanced across the room to where his rifle was leaning in one corner, Victor could keep silence no longer.

"You know what faith we have in you, Deerfoot, but we are anxious, and shall be in distress until we see you back again."

"Why are my brothers troubled?" calmly asked the Shawanoe.

"We can't help believing Taggarak will use treachery, for he must know he isn't certain to win when he attacks you."

"Nothing can make him believe the truth till it comes to him. He will take no warriors with him. Deerfoot is in no danger. Let my brothers smile and be glad."

"I wish I could grin, but it's too hard work," was the doleful response of Victor, the face of his brother showing that he felt the same.

Deerfoot warmly shook hands with each in turn, such being his usual custom, stooped and drew the flap aside and passed from sight. Enough of the Blackfeet were astir to notice him moving at a moderate pace past the lodges toward the clearing at the rear of the village. He greeted all in their own language, and did not show by anything in his manner that he had any important matter in hand. He stealthily glanced here and there, on the lookout for Taggarak, but saw nothing of him. Perhaps the chief had already gone to the scene of the hostile meeting; perhaps he had not yet set out, for the hour was early, or, what was more likely, he had taken another route. Of one thing Deerfoot was certain: the chief had told no one of what was coming, except Mul-tal-la, who bore the message to the youth. When the two combatants should meet, no human eye must witness the terrific combat.

The sagacious Shawanoe had decided to follow a certain line that may impress you as singular for him to adopt. It seemed like undue confidence when he declared that he had no fear of the man who was certainly the most fearful fighter of the whole Blackfoot tribe. Modest as he was by nature, Deerfoot was too intelligent not to understand his decisive superiority, as compared with any of his own or of the white race. That superiority had been proved too often to leave any doubt in his mind. Moreover, with his youth and high health, he was aware that these remarkable powers were not declining, but rather increasing, and ought to increase for a dozen or more years to come.

The American Indian, as a rule, does not show excessive muscular development. Arms and legs are wanting in those ridged bunches of sinew which often bulge out all over our athletes. And yet more than one red man has displayed prodigious strength. Deerfoot believed he was stronger than Taggarak, despite his own light, graceful figure, which made him a dusky Adonis.

He knew that possibly he was mistaken in this respect, but there could be no doubt on another point: he was much quicker of movement than the iron-limbed Taggarak. The open space would give full freedom to both, and this quickness would not be hampered at all during the fight between them. Moreover, Deerfoot was an unerring judge of distance, and knew on the instant when to dodge and when to strike. Therefore he feared not, but with that old Adamic strain in his nature, really yearned for the battle.

It has long been the custom of Indians, when facing each other in mortal strife, to resort to taunts and insults. If a foe can be driven into anger, while his tormentor keeps cool, the latter has the victory half won. Deerfoot could not stifle a feeling of resentment over the contemptuous behavior of Taggarak toward him. Instead of contenting himself with merely challenging the Shawanoe to mortal combat, he sent him word that all that was left for him to do was to choose between two methods of shuffling off the mortal coil. It was to be the Spirit Circle or by the knife of the Blackfoot. This scornful treatment of the youth angered him, and it was one of the reasons why he decided to adopt a policy which in other circumstances he would have considered beneath a true warrior.

CHAPTER XVII.
A MEMORABLE DUEL.

Deerfoot the Shawanoe, before entering the elevated wooded portion to the east of the bleak plain that had been the scene of his triumphs the day before, paused and carefully scrutinized all that lay within his field of vision. He was not altogether free from a shadowy suspicion that Taggarak would resort to treachery, though for reasons named by Mul-tal-la it was improbable. Despite the care the youth had used, he feared that rumors of the coming fight had got abroad, and some of the curious might brave the wrath of their chief for the sake of viewing the combat. That which Deerfoot saw, or rather failed to see, convinced him that both fears were unfounded.

He recalled too clearly the spot named by the Blackfoot to make any mistake, and he went directly to it. A few rods beyond the rocks where Mul-tal-la and Deerfoot had caught sight of each other after their long separation was a comparatively clear and level space that covered a fourth of an acre or less. A glance showed it to be an ideal spot for a meeting such as was at hand.

Deerfoot looked hastily around for Taggarak. He was not in sight. In truth, the Shawanoe was considerably ahead of time, and the chief was not a moment late when, after awhile, he strode into view from the other side of the arena.

This famous chieftain has already been described. No one could look upon him without a certain admiration, and it was easy to believe the many stories of his prowess. He was spare of frame, nearly six feet tall, and his mien and manner showed perfect fearlessness. He wore no head dress, his abundant hair, in which there was not the first streaking of gray, falling loosely over his shoulders, almost to his waist. The upper part of his body was encased in a shirt of deerskin, and the buckskin breeches were fringed down the legs. Deerfoot noticed that he had on a new pair of moccasins, stained several bright colors. He must have thought the occasion warranted something in the nature of display. There was no skirt to the jacket-like garment, the thighs being inclosed with the buckskin which formed the leggings, after the manner of the modern style of trousers. The handle of his knife—the weapon that many a time had done frightful work—could be seen protruding from the girdle that encircled his waist.

With a dignified step the chief strode forward until within a dozen paces of Deerfoot, when he paused and scowled at him.

Following his policy of tantalism, Deerfoot made a mock bow and said:

"Blackfoot, the Shawanoe is glad to see you come at last. But why does the Blackfoot tremble when he finds himself in front of a warrior instead of a squaw who knows not how to fight?"

The chief had never been addressed in this audacious fashion, and his eyes seemed to scintillate from under his scowling brows. Could it be he heard aright?

"When the Shawanoe learned that the Blackfoot who calls himself chief and pretends to be a brave man wished to meet him in fight by this rock, the heart of the Shawanoe was glad and he hurried to come; but the Blackfoot is backward. He hoped the Shawanoe would not come, but he is here and eager to fight him."

And to show the truth of his words, Deerfoot drew his knife from his girdle and grasped it in his good left hand.

Taggarak now found his voice. There was a tremulousness in the words, but it was due to his tumultuous wrath and not to fear.

"Dog of a Shawanoe! Do you choose to die by the hand of Taggarak, or shall he send you to the Spirit Circle? Let him choose!"

"Squaw of a Blackfoot! It shall be *neither*. The Shawanoe cares naught for the Spirit Circle, and will not go there. He has no fear of the Blackfoot who knows how to fight women but trembles when he stands before the Shawanoe! Has the Blackfoot brought some of his warriors to save him from the anger of the Shawanoe?"

And Deerfoot glanced around, as if looking for the help which he knew was not near. He did not see it, but he saw something else, which caused him almost as much displeasure. As he turned toward a large boulder, half hidden by bushes, the upper part of a head dropped down out of sight. Seen only for an instant, the Shawanoe recognized the owner as Victor Shelton, and knew his brother was with him. Despite Deerfoot's orders the boys had managed to steal their way from place to place and were spectators of this meeting. It was too late now to correct the wrong, and he acted as if he knew it not. All the same, he resolved to "discipline" the youths for disregarding his orders.

A Memorable Duel.

In this game of abuse the chief was no match for the Shawanoe, who saw that the tempestuous rage of Taggarak threatened to master him. Accustomed throughout his life to be feared and obeyed, it was unbearable thus to be flouted to his face by a stripling, whom he felt able to crush like a bird's egg. He drew his knife, whose blade was several inches longer than the weapon of the Shawanoe.

With the weapon clinched as if in a vise, the chief thrust his left foot forward for a single pace, but did not advance farther. He was debating with himself how best to dispose of this intolerable youth. A quick death would be too merciful; he would first wound and then prolong his suffering for an hour or more.

"The trembling Blackfoot fears to come to the Shawanoe, so the Shawanoe will go to him."

These words were accompanied with an exquisite sneer, and Deerfoot advanced three paces, taking care to stop before he was within reach of the enraged chief.

"Does the Shawanoe think the God he worships can save him from the vengeance of Taggarak, who spurns that God?"

The reply was a noble one. Dropping his insulting tones and manner, Deerfoot said:

"The Shawanoe knows not whether the God he worships will save him; he never cares nor thinks of *that*. He knows that whatever his Father chooses to do *is right*, and if He does not wish to take care of the Shawanoe, it *is right*. He will go to heaven, the abode of those who obey God, when he is called. He will be ready, whether he hears that call in the gloom of the woods at midnight or on the plain when the sun is high in the sky.

"The Blackfoot worships false gods. Let him learn whether they will help him when he stands in front of the Shawanoe."

The self-confidence of the chief was absolute. Wearied of listening to the taunts of the dusky Apollo, he strode toward him, raising his right hand as he did so, feinted once and then brought down the weapon with a vicious vigor that was meant to bury the point in the shoulder of Deerfoot.

The blade, however, swished through air, and the youth smote the chief squarely in the mouth with the back of his fist. He could have used his knife, but he chose to play awhile with this boaster. He delivered his blow so quickly that the Blackfoot, accustomed as he was to fierce hand-to-hand fighting, had no time to dodge or parry, and the next instant the Shawanoe was ten feet away, weapon still grasped, and grinning at the slightly dazed chief.

"Why does not the Blackfoot squaw strike the Shawanoe? The Shawanoe has struck *him*. Cannot the Blackfoot see where to strike with his knife? He is as slow as an aged woman, but he fears the Shawanoe, who is his master."

Taggarak could not believe his failure was anything more than one of those accidents to which the most skilful fighter is sometimes liable. His weapon was still firm in his hand, and he moved forward again, taking shorter and more stealthy steps. He crouched as if gathering his muscles for a leap, while the Shawanoe contemptuously watched him, alert and observant as a cat.

Six feet away the chief halted. Deerfoot did not stir. Taggarak had learned of the lightning-like quickness of the youth, but felt none the less certain of speedily overcoming him.

For a full minute the two glared at each other, neither speaking, but the same aggravating, scornful smile was on the face of the young Shawanoe. Suddenly he did an astounding thing. He tossed his knife several feet up in the air, caught it by the handle as it came down and then flung it a couple of rods to one side.

"The Shawanoe needs no weapon to conquer the Blackfoot squaw!"

Then Deerfoot voluntarily placed himself in front of the furious warrior, without any weapon with which to defend himself. Not only that, he folded his arms over his breast and with biting irony added:

"Now let the Blackfoot think he has a squaw in front of him; then he will strike hard, if his hand does not tremble."

It was more than flesh and blood could stand. The passion within the breast of the chief broke into a volcano-like flame. With a hissing gasp he sprang forward, striking swiftly with his knife, first downward, then upward and then from side to side, as if he meant to cut the execrated youth into ribbons. He repeated the wild blows with a celerity that almost prevented the eye from following the movements.

But, as before, he split only vacancy. Deerfoot easily eluded the strokes, which were blinder than usual, for Taggarak was beside himself with passion. In the midst of his aimless outburst the Shawanoe did another thing which was worthy of a skilled pugilist. Waiting for an opening, he shot his left hand forward, and, with the open palm, landed a stunning blow on the bridge of the chief's nose. The advantage of such a blow is that, when rightly delivered, tears are forced into the eyes of the one receiving it, who, for a minute or two, is partially blinded. You can understand his fatal position. He cannot pause to clear his vision, for it comes at the crisis of the fight, and an instant halting means ignominious defeat, while to persevere, when he has only the partial use of his sight, makes his disadvantage hardly the less.

While the chief was savagely blinking, in order to enable him to see, the crowning taunt of all sounded in his ears:

"The Blackfoot cries like a pappoose. Does he wish to tread the Spirit Circle? Does he beg the Shawanoe to be merciful to him? If he whines for pity, let him sink on his knees and the Shawanoe will listen to his crying."

Chief Taggarak now lost the last shred of self-control. With a growl of crazy rage he bounded forward again, striking up and down and right and left with a blind, venomous energy that would have exhausted a giant.

Suddenly the wrist which held the whistling blade was seized in the steel-like fingers of Deerfoot's left hand. The grip was fearful, for the Shawanoe had now called upon his last reserve of strength, and the wrist was as if encased in a coil of iron. Then, with a peculiar twist of his hand, known only to himself, and resembling that remarkable system known under the name of jiu jitsu among the Japanese, who are the only ones that understand it in all its frightful perfection, he bent the hand of the chief remorselessly over and backward, until the palm gaped like the mouth of a dying fish and the knife dropped to the ground.

Deerfoot now had both wrists imprisoned. Taggarak gasped and panted and writhed, but could not twist himself loose. In the trial of strength the Shawanoe proved himself the superior. Great drops gathered on the forehead of the Blackfoot. His grin displayed every molar in his head, and the mouth, stretched to double its usual extent, had that horrible appearance when the space between the lips at the corners is the same as in front and the expression is that of a raging wild beast.

Thus the two stood, their arms sawing up and down and from one side to another, without the Blackfoot being able to loosen the merciless grip. He was panting, but no one could have detected any quickening of the respiration of the Shawanoe. His mouth was set and the light of battle flashed in his eyes. He did not speak or yield a point. The crisis had come and he knew he was the victor, just as he knew he would be from the first.

The Blackfoot swayed and his moccasins slid here and there over the ground from the contortion of limbs and body. Then he began pushing with might and main. His eyes were beginning to clear, but the perspiration dripped from the twisted coppery features. Reading his purpose, Deerfoot began pushing also. Neither yielded for a minute or two, and then the chief was slowly forced backward. There was no withstanding the tremendous power of the youth, who strove to the last ounce of his matchless strength.

Taggarak recoiled a step, then another, then began walking backward, and the next minute the walk became a trot on the part of both, the chief retreating and the Shawanoe forcing him faster and faster, though he struggled and resisted with the same panting desperation as at first.

He was still trotting backward with short, increasing steps when Deerfoot, never relaxing his grasp on the writhing wrists, thrust one heel behind his enemy, who tripped and went over. To insure due emphasis in the fall, Deerfoot made a leap as he was going and landed with both knees on the breast of the Blackfoot, who dropped with a thump that forced a gasp from his body and literally shook the earth.

George and Victor Shelton, in their excitement, sprang up from behind the rock that hid them. When Taggarak went over on his back, with Deerfoot bearing him down, Victor could restrain himself no longer. Snatching his cap from his head he swung it aloft, and had opened his mouth to cheer when the slightly less excited brother clapped his hand over his lips.

"What do you mean, you idiot?"

"I want to cheer for Deerfoot! If I don't I'll bust!"

"You will get all the busting you want from him if he finds out we came here, after he told us to stay at home."

"By gracious! That's so; I forgot it. I'm glad you stopped me; we must keep mum. Look!"

CHAPTER XVIII.
DISCIPLINE IN THE RANKS.

The force of the impact and the crushing weight of the Shawanoe's body knocked Taggarak senseless for the moment. He lay panting, with eyes half closed and his countenance glistening with moisture.

Deerfoot, without removing his knees, watched the eyes until they slowly opened and glared upward with a dazed expression. The youth had removed his fingers from the wrist of the chief. He now bent his face close to his and asked:

"Who now is master—the Blackfoot or the Shawanoe? Whose God is the greater—Taggarak's or Deerfoot's?"

But the chieftain was game. He had put up a hurricane fight and had been conquered—conquered by a youth who carried no weapon in his hand, and who could have driven out his life at any moment during the progress of the battle. Instead of slaying his victim, the Shawanoe had put one indignity after another upon him.

"Let the Shawanoe take his knife and kill Taggarak! He does not wish to live!"

"So Taggarak would do with the Shawanoe, but so does not the Shawanoe, for he is a Christian," replied Deerfoot, rising from the prostrate body and stepping back for a couple of paces.

The Blackfoot was still bewildered. He lay motionless for a few seconds, staring at the youth looking serenely down upon him. The chief had been conquered, absolutely, crushingly and to the last degree humiliatingly; for, most amazing thing of all, his conqueror had refused to take his life, knowing that it would have been the other way had the Shawanoe suffered defeat.

And he who showed this unheard-of mercy professed to be a Christian! What a strange religion to make a warrior act in that manner!

Slowly the iron-limbed chieftain climbed to his feet. He was not looking at the Shawanoe, who had folded his arms and was calmly watching him. Taggarak stood upright, turned his face away, took three steps and then paused. His head flirted about like a bird's and he fixed his burning eyes upon the dusky youth, still posed like a statue, with arms folded and on the alert for any treachery.

The Blackfoot gazed steadily into the eyes that met his own without flinching. He did not speak, but, looking away again, strode solemnly across the open space, not pausing to pick up his weapon, and disappeared in the rocky wood.

Deerfoot remained motionless for several moments, gazing at the point where the other had passed from sight. Then he reverently turned his eyes upward and murmured:

"I thank Thee, my Heavenly Father. Thou art kinder to Deerfoot than he deserves."

His next act was most peculiar. He paid no heed to the knife of Taggarak, but picked up his own. It had a keen edge, and instead of thrusting the weapon into his girdle he walked to the nearest undergrowth and began cutting a stick several feet in length and of nearly an inch's thickness at the butt.

About this time George and Victor Shelton, from their hiding place, where they had stealthily watched everything, began to feel disturbed in mind.

"What do you suppose he is doing that for?" whispered Victor, peeping around the corner of the rock.

"I'm blessed if I know. He is trimming off the twigs, so as to make the stick smooth."

"Do you suppose he saw us?"

"He couldn't. He has mighty sharp eyes, but he had no chance to look anywhere except in the face of Taggarak, and we haven't shown ourselves since he left."

"It's a queer performance anyway, and I don't feel—"

"Sh! He's looking this way."

The next moment both boys shivered, for, facing the rock which until then they were certain had hid them from view, the Shawanoe called:

"Let my brothers come here. Deerfoot wishes to speak to them."

"He saw us after all!" gasped Victor. "Let's run!"

"What good will that do? There's no getting away from him."

"He looks savage, George; he means business. Can't we combine and lick him if he tries to play smart with us?"

"If we could get Mul-tal-la and three or four other Blackfeet we might have a show; but it would take more than you and me to down him. Come, it won't do to wait any longer."

The brothers were pretty well convinced of what was coming and were scared. To Victor only one possible escape presented itself—that was to conciliate the Shawanoe. The lad made a brave attempt to do so.

Coming out from behind the rock, he strode rapidly down the gentle slope, as if he had just recognized the youth. Victor's face was aglow, and he certainly meant all he said:

"I tell you, Deerfoot, that was the greatest victory you ever won! I don't believe the man ever lived that downed Taggarak, and yet you did it without any weapon. People won't believe the story, but you can refer them to us. Ain't it lucky, now, that we happened to be where we could see you lay out that boasting chief?"

George caught at the straw thus held out by his brother.

"I tell you that's so, Deerfoot. The news of this fight is bound to get out sooner or later. Some who don't know you won't believe anything of the kind, till we tell them we saw the whole business and it was just as you say. Ain't you glad, Deerfoot, we happened by chance to be where we could see it all?"

The Shawanoe had thrust his knife into his girdle and held the switch firmly by its larger end. He looked gravely into the face of each lad while he was speaking. When they ceased he had something to say:

"When Deerfoot and his brothers left Woodvale was it not said that the Shawanoe should rule and guide them?"

"There can't be any question of *that*," Victor promptly replied.

"And my brothers promised to obey him in all things?"

"It seems to me I remember something of that kind."

"Has Deerfoot been a hard master?"

"We couldn't have had a kinder one. I tell you, Deerfoot, you know more in five minutes than George and I know in a month, or ever will know. We couldn't get along without you. We have been pretty obedient, as a rule, haven't we?"

"Was not the agreement between Taggarak and Deerfoot that no person should look upon the fight between them?"

"Yes; but I don't believe Taggarak kept his promise."

Deerfoot flashed a look of inquiry at Victor.

"What does my brother mean by his words? Did he see any other Blackfoot near?"

"Well, not exactly; but there were marks in the bushes which looked as if made by moccasins. I shouldn't wonder if some were hiding there and ran away when they saw us coming and knew we meant to see you had fair play."

The appeal was wasted. Deerfoot took his station between the brothers, moving them apart so they were separated by a space of five or six feet. He then deliberately, vigorously and impartially laid the switch over the shoulders of George and Victor. You would not suspect the vim with which this disciplining was carried out. Only the brothers themselves could testify feelingly as to that.

And the boys had to "grin and bear it," for there was no escape for them. It was useless to run, and had they tried it they would have been punished more severely. They were too proud to complain. The quicker-tempered Victor wanted to revolt and attack the Shawanoe, but he knew George would not join him, for such rebellion would have been disastrous to them. They had tested the ability of Deerfoot in that line too often to doubt his superiority. Had the shadow of a doubt lingered, the scene they had witnessed a few minutes before would have dispelled it.

The rod descended first upon the shoulders of Victor, then upon those of George, and there was no difference in the force of the blows. Oh, how they stung! Each boy wanted to scratch the smarting parts, but grimly stood it out. Finally Victor ventured to say:

"When you are tired, Deerfoot, you have our permission to stop."

"Tired! He won't get tired in a week. Our only hope is that he will use up all the switches in the country."

And the Shawanoe kept at it till the rod broke in the middle and only the stump was left in his hand. He flung that aside, and, without speaking, turned and walked toward the village. As soon as his face was turned the boys devoted their efforts to rubbing and scratching their arms, shoulders and backs.

"How many times do you think he struck us?" ruefully asked George.

"I guess about four thousand; but I forgot to count."

"He started in with you and ended with me, so we both got the same. Gracious alive, but he knows his business!"

"Anyhow, what we saw was worth all we had to pay. I didn't think he would do anything of the kind, did you?"

"No; I thought we might keep our visit a secret, but not many things escape his eye. I suppose after all he was right."

"Wait till these smarts let up a little before you ask me to say that," replied Victor, still rubbing and fidgeting about. "Can't you think of some way of getting even with him?"

"I wish I could, but the worst thing anyone can do is to tackle Deerfoot. We must try to believe we were lucky in getting off as lightly as we did."

"Lightly!" sniffed Victor. "I should like to know what you call *heavy* if that is light."

"And he is still mad at us. He went off without speaking, and it may be days before he gets over his anger."

Bye and bye the smarts so subsided that the boys felt comparatively comfortable. As they picked their way homeward their resentment cooled, and they were able to see things in their proper light. They profoundly loved and admired the young Shawanoe, and required no one to remind them of his affection for them. The punishment he had administered was like that of a father to a wayward child. Moreover, it was well deserved, and they were willing to confess the fact before they reached their tepee.

"There's no getting out of it," said the more impulsive Victor. "He forbade us to follow him, and it was breaking the agreement between him and Taggarak. The only thing for us to do when we meet him again is to say we are sorry and ask his forgiveness. I'm ready to do so. Are you, George?"

"Why didn't we try that on him before he gave us the whipping?"

"It wouldn't have worked. When I saw him cutting and trimming that switch I knew what was coming, and there was no way for us to dodge it."

"It seems pretty hard, after a fellow has had his life almost whaled out of him, to say he is sorry. It seems to me it's the other chap who ought to feel sorry."

"No, we were in the wrong and must apologize. You know how tender-hearted Deerfoot is. I believe he felt pity for Taggarak, even though he knew the chief meant to kill him. The Blackfoot isn't the first enemy Deerfoot has had at his mercy and then spared him."

When the boys reached their lodge, after meeting and greeting a number of their dusky friends, they were disappointed not to find Deerfoot there. He did not come in until late in the afternoon. He raised the robe at the door, glanced at the brothers, but kept his lips closed. Victor walked up to him without a moment's hesitation and extended his hand:

"Deerfoot, you served us right. We are both sorry. Will you forgive us?"

The two saw the moisture creep into the handsome dark eyes and noted the tremor of the Shawanoe's voice as he took each hand in turn and said:

"Yes, Deerfoot forgives you. We are brothers again."

CHAPTER XIX.
"BEHOLD HE PRAYETH."

Mul-tal-la the Blackfoot obeyed the command of Taggarak, his chief. But though he kept away from the meeting place of the duelists, he hovered not far off, in order to learn at the earliest possible moment the result of the most important personal encounter that had ever taken place in the history of the Blackfoot nation. Because of the circuitous course taken by George and Victor Shelton, Mul-tal-la saw nothing of them and never learned of the humorous appendix to the tragedy.

The sight of the Shawanoe returning told who was victor, and a few brief words between the two, as they met, made known that he had spared the life of the chief, who slunk silently off in the solitude, no one but himself knew whither. It was this flight that was on the mind of Deerfoot and Mul-tal-la, for each felt that momentous consequences were to flow therefrom.

The four friends were once more gathered in the home of the guests of the Blackfoot tribe. Each knew a crisis was at hand that might compel them, on the edge of the severe northern winter, to depart for other quarters, and the flight, perhaps, would become impossible because of the ferocious rage of the humiliated chieftain.

The Shelton brothers acted the part of listeners, sensibly feeling that they could contribute nothing to the discussion between Mul-tal-la and Deerfoot; but no speakers could have asked for more deeply interested auditors than they.

"Taggarak has not come back," said the Blackfoot. "Mul-tal-la stopped at his lodge, and his squaw said she had seen naught of him since this morning."

"She does not know what took place?" was the inquiring remark of Deerfoot.

"She could not, for he kept his word and told no one before, and," grimly added the Blackfoot, "he would not tell anyone afterward."

"What does she think?"

"That he has gone to one of the other villages. Taggarak is a silent man, and he sometimes departs in the middle of the night, without saying a word to anyone. He may be gone for weeks, and no one here will know anything of it until he returns."

"What does Mul-tal-la think?"

"He knows not what to think. If Taggarak is not here to-morrow, then he will believe the chief is visiting his other warriors."

"Does he not summon his other chiefs to come to him?"

"Often; they meet at the Big Lodge. They talk together, when they are making ready to go on raids among other tribes, and Taggarak gives them his commands; but he likes to appear in their villages when they do not look for his coming. What does my brother believe the chief will do when he comes back?"

The Shawanoe waited for a minute or two before replying:

"There is a mist in the eyes of Deerfoot and he cannot see clearly. Taggarak is brave but cruel. He will not rest under his overthrow. Deerfoot thinks they will have to fight again."

"And will Deerfoot spare him once more?"

"He cannot answer. He will do as God tells him to do."

Victor Shelton felt that this was a good time for him to add to the discussion.

"Mul-tal-la, do you think it is possible Taggarak wants to fight Deerfoot, after he has been beaten by him? Why should he want to try it again?"

"Because he has hope of winning the fight."

"He can't have any such hope. Why, Deerfoot whipped him without a weapon in his hand, while Taggarak had his big, ugly knife most of the time."

Mul-tal-la had not heard anything of this, and he looked inquiringly at Deerfoot and then at the boy who had made the amazing statement. Victor flushed and stammeringly added:

"That is—it would have been easy for Deerfoot to whip him without any weapon and with one hand tied behind his back—that is, it looks so to me and George—and I'm sure he could do it if he wished—confound it, Deerfoot, *didn't* you whip him as I said?"

The visitor turned to the Shawanoe, who gravely nodded his head.

"Deerfoot has told me things from the good book which he carries with him, and he said there was One who used to do some things so strange that they were called miracles."

"Yes, He did many of them."

"Then Deerfoot did a miracle if he overthrew Taggarak without the help of any weapon."

"No," modestly replied the Shawanoe, "there was no miracle. It was easier to defeat him without a weapon than with one. Deerfoot wrenched the knife from his hand and then threw him to the ground; that was all."

"That was all!" repeated the Blackfoot, as if to himself. Then he looked at the boys and the three laughed.

"Yes, that was all. George or I could have done the same, but we thought it better to turn the job over to Deerfoot. He's fond of doing such trifles," said Victor, airily.

The result of the conference was the decision that naught could be done except to await the issue of events. All feared the worst, and strove to prepare for it. The belief was that the rage in the breast of Chief Taggarak would lead him to merciless measures, not only against his visitors, but against all of his own people who had showed an inclination to embrace the new religion.

Three days passed and nothing was heard of the chief. He was still absent, and the general belief of his people that he was among the other villages averted misgiving. Only those in the secret were in dread. But the seed planted by Deerfoot began to bear fruit. Inquiries came to him, and the excitement over the religion he brought, even though subdued, spread among the warriors and women of the tribe. Finally Mul-tal-la came to him with the surprising request that he would address the Indians in the Big Lodge on the all-important subject. In making the request, Mul-tal-la the Blackfoot spoke for others. Without hesitation the Shawanoe replied that he would do as desired. He felt it was his duty, and he was the last one to shrink.

Near the middle of the primitive settlement was a structure known as the "Big Lodge." It was of the simplest build, being some forty feet in length by about half that width. It consisted of upright poles at the corners, with other supports along the sides, and a roof of boughs similar to that of the royal lodge. All the sides were open; there were no seats and no provisions for fire. Consequently the temperature was always the same as that outdoors.

It was the custom of the Blackfeet to hold their councils in this place, Taggarak being fond of summoning his chiefs and leading warriors thither, while they smoked their pipes and settled questions of state. Most of the time the barren structure was deserted.

On a bleak afternoon late in autumn, when a few inches of snow lay on the ground and the wind moaned among the leafless branches, Deerfoot the Shawanoe and the Shelton brothers wended their way to the Big Lodge. The boys paused at the edge of the assemblage and silently took their place among the listeners. They, as well as their friend, were astonished to see the crowd that had gathered. Warriors and women, with here and there a child, were seated everywhere on the bare ground, till it was hard to find room for another person. No one could fail to be impressed by the air of solemnity that shadowed each dusky face. Nearly every male and female sat with a shawl wrapped around the shoulders, for the air was biting, and no one had any protection from it except clothing. Victor whispered to his brother:

"I never expected to see anything like this. Who would have thought that the few words Deerfoot has spoken about our religion could have stirred up such deep feeling?"

An Indian scorns to betray curiosity or excitement, and only a few of the warriors and squaws looked up as the young Shawanoe picked his way through and among the multitude, who numbered several hundred, to the farther end of the space, where he turned to face the expectant listeners. He had left his rifle at the tepee, but his knife was in his girdle. To those who had slight knowledge of him he looked his simple, natural self; but George and Victor, when they scanned their friend observed a deeper flush in his face and a brighter gleam in the eyes, which revealed to them the profound emotion that stirred his soul.

Deerfoot stood for a minute, looking over the swarthy faces turned expectantly toward him. He had prayed many times for strength to meet this ordeal, and he knew he would do so.

Then he began speaking in his low, musical voice, which was clearly heard by those farthest removed. He used the Blackfoot tongue, so that only a part of his words were understood by George and Victor, and never halted or hesitated until the interruption came.

"My friends," said he, "the heart of Deerfoot is glad to tell you about the Great Spirit who is the Father of the red men as well as of the palefaces. Many, many moons ago that Father made this world; the sun that shines by day and the moon and stars that rule at night; the mountains, the woods, the rivers, the prairies, the rocks, the clouds and all that you see about you. He gave His children game to hunt, and He caused the fish to grow in the streams and the corn and fruit to spring from the ground. There was nothing that His children needed that He did not give to them.

"Was not that Father kind? Could any father be as good to his children as God was to those He put on the earth to live together? Should not those children love Him and try to live as He wished them to live? But they were wicked and did not care for Him. They fought and killed one another and did all they could to offend their Heavenly Father. They were so bad that bye and bye He turned away His face in anger. He would have slain them as they deserved, but He had a Son, good and pure like Himself. This Son took the load of all the sins of the world on his heart. He came to the earth and told the people how sad God was because they did evil. Some heeded His words, but bad men took the Son, whom we call our Saviour, because He saved us all—you and me and everybody—and they drove nails through his hands and feet, and let Him hang on two crosspieces of wood till He died the most painful of deaths. He could have killed those who treated Him so cruelly, but He chose to die so that the way would be opened for all men and women and children to come to God, who was angry no longer, because the Son had taken their place and suffered in their stead.

"The Great Spirit, whom we call God or our Heavenly Father, has made the path so straight and so free from briars that the smallest child can walk therein without harm. He wants you to become Christians and to believe in Him. A

Christian is one who does all he can to make others happy. You must not go to war, and only fight when others attack you or those whom you love. You must be merciful and forgiving. Never cause anyone to suffer. Give food to the hungry, help those who have fallen to climb to their feet, take them by the hand and lead them if they are weak. Think all the time of new ways of making other persons smile. You must pray to God every morning and night and, when you have the chance, through the day. If you do this, a sweet peace, such as you have never known before, will come into your heart. You will not care for pain or hunger or thirst or suffering, for the happiness of pleasing your Heavenly Father will make you forget all these. When you die He will carry you to those blessed hunting grounds, where you shall meet all the friends who have gone on before and where you and they shall be happy forevermore."

During the utterance of this simple plea the Big Lodge was as still as the tomb. It is safe to believe that not a man or woman present failed to be impressed, for every person, savage or civilized, pagan or Christian, is profoundly interested in the most transcendant theme that can engage the human mind—the saving of man's soul and the preparation for the life to come. None other can compare with it. It is the one supreme question of the ages.

Those who looked at Deerfoot thought he had finished his address, but it was not so. George and Victor Shelton were the first to understand from his manner that something outside of the lodge had checked him. He was looking beyond the boys at some object that had made him cease speaking. The boys turned their heads to learn the meaning of the interruption. As they did so they heard some one approaching with a rapid step.

It was Taggarak, the chief, his face aflame, his stride long and rapid and his intense gaze centered on the young Shawanoe. Paying no heed to those in his way, he brushed past, overturning several and plowed straight through the crowd toward Deerfoot, who calmly awaited his coming.

Every eye was fixed upon the terrible chieftain, and hardly one of his people doubted that he meant to assail the Shawanoe. The hearts of George and Victor Shelton stood still, for they felt that a tragedy was about to open.

Instead of drawing his knife, Deerfoot placed both hands behind his back, after the idle manner of one who feels little interest in what is going on before him.

Within a couple of paces of Deerfoot, Taggarak wheeled around, and, in a voice of thunder addressed his people:

"The Shawanoe speaks with a single tongue! His words are true! The Great Spirit he tells you about is the true and only Great Spirit! Taggarak did not think so; he scorned him, but his eyes have been opened and he now sees. He has been wandering in the woods for days and nights, trying to flee from the anger of that Great Spirit. His eyes were filled with tears; he lay on his face and cried to Him; he did not eat nor drink nor sleep; but the Great Spirit, the true Great Spirit, spoke loving words to Taggarak. He raised him to his feet; He showed him that all the briars had been taken from his path. Taggarak looked around and all the darkness was gone and the sun was shining in the sky. The Great Spirit was pleased. He told Taggarak he was now His son and all shall be well with him.

"Heed the words of the Shawanoe, for they are true. Taggarak is a Christian and wishes all the Blackfeet to become Christians."

CHAPTER XX.
LIGHT IN DARKNESS.

It must not be thought that the large assemblage which had gathered in the Big Lodge were of one mind, or even that a majority were ready to accept the new religion that was explained to them by its model exemplar, Deerfoot the Shawanoe. A few yearned for the light, and had already learned enough of the elemental truths to be drawn toward them; but the majority were attracted by that potent cause—curiosity. They listened closely. The simple words of the preacher showed clearly that the new faith was the opposite of the old; that, if accepted by them, it meant a revolution in their beliefs and practices.

Most of the men and a few of the women revolted at the thought. To them the most powerful of motives in human conduct were those of revenge, of prowess in battle, and of mercilessness toward an enemy. To be told that they must root out this passion and be governed by the Golden Rule was turning themselves into squaws, and spurning that nobility which is the crowning glory of the red man's life. Their demeanor was stolid. The wise Deerfoot plainly saw, however, that his doctrine found favor with only a few. He made his appeal as clear and direct as he knew how, but he did not need to be told that he was only partially successful.

The dramatic entrance and declaration by Chief Taggarak of the "pangs of transformation" through which he had passed and his emergence into the new light could not fail to be impressive and to add to the force of what had just been said by the Shawanoe. None the less, it had also an opposite effect in some cases. The warriors who had accepted the leadership for years of one of the greatest chiefs that ever swayed the destinies of the Blackfoot people now repudiated him. He upon whom they had relied so long to lead them in battle and of whose unquestioned bravery and prodigious prowess all knew, had become a woman! But *they* would remain true warriors and maintain the prestige of their tribe as among the most aggressive in the Northwest.

Still Taggarak swept a number with him. Probably when he was through with his burning appeal a fifth of those present were under "conviction," and could be counted upon in favorable circumstances to become believers in the faith preached by the One who spake and taught as never man spake and taught. It may be said that a half of that number were resolute in this decision. Their sentiments were crystallized. The seed had been sown on good ground and was bearing fruit.

The young Shawanoe was tactful. For him to attempt to add anything to the words of Taggarak would be to weaken them. They were the climax, and silence was golden. Throughout the eloquent appeal of the chief, Deerfoot stood with his hands idly folded behind him, his eyes fixed upon the face of Taggarak, whose pose gave a good view of his features, and listening in the very intentness of his soul. When the chief had uttered his last word he gathered his blanket about his shoulders and strode out of the Big Lodge, looking neither to the right nor left, and again failing to notice his wife and little boy, who sat on the ground and whom he brushed as he passed into the open air. He did not glance behind, but continued his dignified, deliberate stride till he was hidden from sight among the trees beyond the cleared space.

Before this, Deerfoot, without speaking a word, picked his way through the throng, who surveyed him curiously but did not stir until he was outside. The Shawanoe glanced at George and Victor Shelton, and by a look indicated that they were to follow him. They did so, silent like the others, and the three returned to their own tepee without exchanging a word on the road. They were awed by what they had seen and heard, and respected their friend too much to break in upon his meditations. He sat down on the furs in his usual place and they busied themselves with what may be considered their household duties, speaking only now and then to each other. The afternoon was drawing to a close, and, but for the fire that was kept burning, it would have been dark within the lodge. They prepared their meal, but when Deerfoot was invited to eat he shook his head, rose to his feet and passed out.

The Shawanoe had no more time than to straighten up in the open air when he was face to face with Mul-tal-la, who was on his way to see him. They pressed each other's hand and the visitor said:

"Chief Taggarak wishes that his brother the Shawanoe shall come to his lodge."

"Deerfoot goes there," replied the youth, who had been meditating doing so. "Will my brother go with Deerfoot?"

"Only to the lodge. Taggarak does not wish to see *him*."

The two walked side by side, the hearts of both full. It was so dark that they drew no attention to themselves. Just before the well-known home of the chief was reached, Mul-tal-la turned off without so much as a farewell word.

The war chief was expecting his visitor. He had sent his wife and boy away in order that he might be alone with the Shawanoe. He sat with his back against the rock, his position allowing the firelight to show his face clearly, especially one side of it. As he recognized his visitor he smiled and extended his hand, after the manner of white men. Deerfoot quickened his pace and grasped the palm and laid the other on the shoulder of the chieftain. How different from their meeting by the lookout rock several days before!

"The heart of Deerfoot is glad," said the visitor, in a low, tremulous voice.

"Taggarak hears the birds sing again. There are no clouds before the sun. He is happy, for the Great Spirit smiles upon him."

One of the most marvelous facts connected with the true religion, and itself a proof of its divinity, is its complete adaptability to every condition of life and to every degree of intelligence. Its essentials are as readily grasped by the clodhopper as by the profoundest scholar whose years are spent in delving into the mysteries of science. No finite mind can fathom the mysteries of life, of death, of sleep, of the beginning, the end, of eternity, of the real nature of the soul and of God, how He came into existence; nor, indeed, shall we ever comprehend in all their fullness the simplest phenomena around us. What is the essence of color or taste or smell? How is the word spoken by us understood by him to whom it is addressed? When we move a hand or foot, where and how does the action *begin*? What is the theoretical limit of divisibility or expansion? These and scores of similar questions have only to be asked for us to feel the utter helplessness of our powers of understanding.

But to the untutored savage, shivering in his rude wigwam and manacled by his sombre superstitions, the essential facts for the saving of his soul become as clear as the sun in the unclouded heavens. The man with a dwarfed intellect can see as plainly as he whose telescope, sweeping the heavens, carries his vision to the bounds of the universe.

"All our philosophic pedants, all our sons of science know
Not a whit more than that dullard knew a million years ago."

Deerfoot stayed with Taggarak for several hours. No one disturbed them, and the chief would have kept his comforter still longer had not the latter felt that it was better to leave the Blackfoot to his communings with God.

When at last the Shawanoe emerged like a shadow from the lodge of the chief he did not go to his own home. Instead, he turned off, passed swiftly across the open space that had been the scene of so many contests and games, entered the hilly section and did not pause until he came to the place where he and Taggarak had fought several days before.

Deerfoot had left his rifle at home and was alone. Folding his arms and standing on the very spot where he had flung Taggarak to the earth and held him at his mercy, he looked up at the faintly moonlit sky and murmured:

"Deerfoot does not deserve such happiness as now fills his heart. He thanks God for His mercy."

Never in all his brief but eventful career had the young Shawanoe felt more unmistakably the presence of the Father whom he worshiped and strove to obey. Ambition gratified, triumph obtained, earthly love, physical or mental achievements, defeat of opponents, wealth, pleasure, gratification of taste and longings, all these combined cannot give to the human soul that thrilling happiness which kindles and glows and burns into life when Conscience whispers, "Well done!" and we know that some thought or word or deed of ours is pleasing to God.

Nothing was or could be more real to Deerfoot than the cause of the radiance that suffused his being when he came from the lodge of the Blackfoot chieftain. Science may try to explain such emotions as an exaltation resulting from physical causes, but no such explanation can suffice. We feel that which we feel and know that which we know.

CHAPTER XXI.
HOMEWARD BOUND.

Despite the remarkable experiences of George and Victor Shelton in the Blackfoot village, they found, as the weeks and months passed, a monotony that deepened their homesickness and caused them to yearn for the day when they could start southward and leave the bleak region forever behind. The winters in that latitude are generally severe, and the brothers got a taste of cold weather such as they had never known on the other side of the Mississippi. There must have been repeated spells when, had a Fahrenheit thermometer been in existence, it would have shown a record of thirty and forty degrees below zero.

People who are accustomed to such Arctic experiences know how to prepare for them, and Deerfoot and the boys would have been foolish had they neglected so plain a duty. With wood abundant on every hand, a bountiful supply was kept within the tepee and outside, and weeks passed without the fire being allowed to go out. With the soft, warm furs at command, no one of the three met with more than a brief discomfort because of the fearful cold.

The chief cause of anxiety was the horses. All were provided with shelter and carefully looked after. A good deal of grass had been pulled and much cottonwood and willow bark laid in stock. If the animals could not fare sumptuously, they had enough to keep them in good condition. Fully half a dozen of the Blackfoot horses were frozen to death, and those belonging to our friends would have perished but for the care they received. They were screened by blankets during the unusually severe weather, and Whirlwind received the tenderest attention from Deerfoot. More than once the Shawanoe stole out of the tepee in the depth of the night and tramped over the snow through an atmosphere that was still and as biting as the teeth of a saw. No matter how silently the youth moved forward, the stallion discovered his approach and whinneyed his welcome. Then when the blizzards raged Deerfoot never forgot to call and assure himself that nothing was neglected that could shield the faithful creatures. Thus they were saved from harm until the weather moderated upon the approach of spring.

With the snow lying several feet deep on the level and piled ten times higher among the mountains, Deerfoot and the boys hunted with their friends on snowshoes. It was exhilarating, but the resistless cold took away much of the pleasure that otherwise would have come to the lads. As for the Shawanoe, summer and winter seemed alike to him.

When the village was helpless in the grasp of old Boreas, the inhabitants did little except cower in their lodges around their fires and eat and sleep. This sort of existence grew almost intolerable to the brothers. With every muscle and nerve yearning for action, they became impatient and sometimes fretful. When they spoke of themselves as prisoners it was the truth.

Taggarak acted kindly toward George and Victor, but never showed any special friendship for them. It may have been because they belonged to another race. Toward Deerfoot he displayed a profound gratitude, a deep affection and reverence, amounting at times almost to worship. He was the messenger who brought the glad tidings of the one and only true God, and the chief in some way or other associated him with the divine message itself, as if he were a part of it.

The snow and cold shut off communication almost entirely between the Blackfoot villages. Early in the winter and toward spring several warriors came down from the most northern settlement, but they did not remain long. It was known, however, among them all that Taggarak, the leading chief, had accepted the new religion, and his authority naturally weakened, but nothing in the nature of a revolt took place against his supremacy.

Deerfoot frequently visited the chief, where none was so welcome as he. Taggarak never went to the tepee of the Shawanoe, for he preferred always to see Deerfoot alone. Mul-tal-la, Spink, Jiggers and seven other warriors openly confessed the Christian religion. Nearly double that number of squaws—among them the wife of the chief—did the same. Slowly and surely the leaven worked, and when the time drew near for the departure of the visitors it is probable that the number of converts was doubled, with the promise of further increase.

Deerfoot and the boys made the parting as "informal" as possible. All through the winter the Shawanoe had impressed upon the Blackfeet that this separation in the nature of things would be brief. The time was certain to come, at no distant day, when they would all be together again. So he smiled, the boys bade good-bye to the numerous lads with whom they had played and hunted, and were so happy over the prospect of soon seeing their own home again that they could not repress their delight nor pay much attention to the regret, if not sadness, of the aboriginal youngsters.

Deerfoot's last hour in the village was spent alone with Taggarak in his lodge. What took place there and what was said by each were never known to anyone beside themselves.

By the middle of the afternoon our friends had penetrated a number of miles to the eastward. A good deal of snow remained, and they had to pick their way with care. They would have been wise had they remained another month, as they were urged to do; but Deerfoot himself was as homesick as his companions and as willing as they to face the hardships that had to be faced for several weeks to come.

Jack, Prince, Zigzag and even Whirlwind showed the effects of their long confinement, but all appeared to share the enthusiasm of their owners and worked royally to get forward. When they had traveled the distance named, the rest given them by their masters was not unwelcome.

Naturally, upon halting, all turned their eyes westward. A moderate mountain spur hid the village from sight, but each knew where it lay. George and Victor scanned the field of vision with the aid of the glass, but noted nothing unusual. When Deerfoot took the instrument he stood for a long time directed toward a certain spot. He expected to see some object, and was not disappointed. On the top of the same bare brown rock where he had caught sight of Mul-tal-la when Deerfoot was coming to the village for the first time, he descried another form. It was not that of Mul-tal-la; it was Taggarak, who had climbed alone to the place, and, silent and motionless as a statue, was gazing after the little party of horsemen as they slowly faded from view in the distance.

George and Victor kept their eyes on their friend, and when they noted the length of time he held the glass leveled they suspected the cause.

"He sees some one," said George, in a low tone.

"It must be Taggarak. Look!"

Deerfoot had lowered the instrument and was peering westward with his unaided vision. He was testing whether he could thus discern that which the glass revealed plainly. Evidently he did so, though the boys could not locate the form, even when they knew almost precisely where to look for it.

Standing upright, the Shawanoe took his blanket from the back of Whirlwind and swung it back and forth over his head, for fully a dozen times. Then, dropping it to his feet, he brought the glass again to his eye.

"Taggarak has seen it," whispered Victor, who, like his brother, was watching the face of Deerfoot and noted the smile come to his countenance.

Such was the fact. As the Shawanoe looked again he observed the chieftain rise from his sitting position and reply to the signal by waving his own blanket. The trained vision of the veteran warrior saw as clearly as those of youth. The action of Taggarak brought him into view of the lads, both noting the flickering of what resembled a mere speck in the distance. Finally, Deerfoot lowered the glass and turned about, as if to say that was the final parting from the chief who held him in such loving remembrance.

The mountain peaks on every hand were covered with snow. On the lower ranges this would gradually dissolve under the rays of the sun, but others were so lofty that the white blanket remained throughout the year. While gazing at a towering range to the northeast the three witnessed the descent of an avalanche. Deerfoot was the first to see it, and directed the notice of the boys to the vast disturbance.

The glance revealed nothing unusual, the enormous extent of slope looking as if it were motionless, but a second look told the truth. A grove of pines at the base of the range were suddenly snuffed out. This was because they disappeared under the prodigious mass of snow and ice that swept over them. Then a dark, irregular line, running right and left, and roughly parallel with the crest of the range, came into view. It was an eighth of a mile in length and the narrow width rapidly increased until there was a rent or yawn of several hundred feet, zigzagging from one side to the other. The dark color of this chasm was due to rocks and ground, and marked the break between the two sections or divisions of the avalanche. The upper portion caught and held, while the remainder swept downward without check. Thus a huge gap was opened, through which the brown earth and stones showed.

The next strange sight was that of boulders, some of them weighing many tons, flung high in air and tossed about like so many corks. One might have thought that Titans were disporting themselves as did the fabled gods on Mount Olympus. As the inconceivable mountain of snow crashed onward it spread out at the base of the range, and finally settled to rest. Had an ordinary town been in its path it would have been buried to the tops of the highest steeples.

Nearly all this had taken place before the three spectators heard the deep, thunderous roar that rolled across the space and told of the stupendous mass that had been loosened by the undermining rays of the sun or by some trifling disturbance of the atmosphere.

"If we should be caught in anything like that," said Victor, "it would take us a good while to dig out."

"My brothers might *never* dig out," said Deerfoot.

"What is there to hinder?"

"There are many stones and rocks and boulders tumbling about in the snow, and they would be likely to kill us."

"Then, Deerfoot, you must keep your eyes open for avalanches. It would be pretty hard for the horses, though Zigzag has sort of got used to it."

Little need for warning the Shawanoe of his duty. That was what he had been attending to all his life. He had never placed himself and friends in the way of an impending avalanche. Recalling their course since leaving the village, the brothers understood better than before the cause of more than one tortuous winding by their guide, when they had been unable to guess the reason for such quixotic turns that did not lessen the labor of traveling itself.

It was not yet midday, and the halt was not made for food for either man or beast. In truth, grass was so scarce, except here and there in the sheltered nooks and depressions, that some dependence would have to be placed for awhile on the barks of trees. Zigzag showed a meekness that roused distrust on the part of the boys. He must have found the heavy pack quite onerous, but he did not rebel. Whirlwind showed little lessening of his aristocratic tastes, and refused to mingle on anything like equal terms with the common stock around him.

When Deerfoot and his companions were journeying westward they decided to return by a different route from the Blackfoot country. Their first intention was to travel eastward until they reached the upper waters of the Mississippi, and then make their way down that stream to civilization, following in a general way the course of the mighty stream. With their horses, and without large boats, they could not utilize the current, unless perhaps after descending a long distance they were able to construct a large raft.

This plan, which would have taken them through the hunting grounds of the Assiniboines, was changed, and they turned to the southeast, having been told that that course offered less difficulties to them. They gave up their former plan because of their wish to enter a moderate climate as soon as possible. Although spring was well begun, they had a good deal of snow and ice to encounter, and were likely to meet it for weeks to come. This was shown on their second day, when a driving storm of snow and sleet forced them to seek shelter for themselves and horses, and another day passed before they could resume their journey.

The most trying difficulty was that of crossing streams, which were more numerous than they had supposed. Some were mountain torrents of only a few yards width, others deserved the name of rivers, and the current of each was of icy coldness. More than once they saw blocks of ice grinding and tumbling over one another as they plunged rapidly onward. It was so dangerous at times for the horses to attempt to swim across, and so hard and disagreeable for the youths, that hours were spent in hunting for a fording place. Fortunately they were always able to gather enough fuel to make themselves comfortable at night; grass became more plentiful and no trouble was had in procuring game. This generally consisted of bison, but it was a great improvement when they were able to bring down a Rocky Mountain sheep. This animal does not bear wool, but hair like that of the deer, and is larger than the largest domestic sheep. The horns of the males attain great size, starting from just above the eyes, though not touching at the bases, and curving over so as to include all the space between the ears. The meat at certain seasons is very palatable and held in high favor. The animal is generally known by the name of the "big horn," and is so skilful a climber and so alert that it is quite a feat for a hunter to bring down a specimen. Deerfoot was the only one on this return journey who was able to bag the game, which never failed to elude George and Victor Shelton.

CHAPTER XXII.
A MEMORABLE MEETING.

If you will examine the map of the State of Montana you will note that the central county bears the name of Fergus, while one of the counties lying directly south is Yellowstone. The boundary between these two is the Musselshell River, which, flowing directly northward, separates Custer and Dawson counties, joining the Missouri at the northeastern corner of Fergus County. It was in the latter part of May, 1805, that Deerfoot and the two Shelton boys, after a long, wearisome ride and tramp through a wild and unknown region, broken by mountain spurs and crossed by numberless streams, arrived at the mouth of the Musselshell.

Even with summer hardly a fortnight off, ice formed at night, flurries of snow filled the air at times and the camp fire became a necessity. And yet our friends were plagued by mosquitoes, grass was plentiful, and there was no lack of game. The party seemed to be sharing the summer and winter seasons, with the most disagreeable features of both.

Having followed the Missouri so far, Deerfoot said that a crossing place must be found before the morrow, for it was inevitable that the farther they went down stream the larger it would become, because of its numerous tributaries. The Missouri was an eighth of a mile across at its junction with the Musselshell, but its current was gentle. Not an Indian had been seen for four days, and Deerfoot was on foot searching the northern shore for a good crossing place when George Shelton called out:

"Look! There are white men on the other side of the river!"

Deerfoot had observed them and had halted and scrutinized them with no little interest and wonder. The first sight was of six or eight men coming round a bend in the Missouri, all having hold of a long elk-skin rope which, passing over the shoulder of each, was fastened to a large pirogue. Directly behind them was a similar boat, and then six small canoes, the whole string being towed by fully a score of men. The boats contained a large amount of luggage, while a dozen men, one of whom was a negro servant, took turns at the labor.

Since the afternoon was drawing to a close the party came to a pause, and the next minute were looking across the stream at the three youths with their four animals, the riders having dismounted, each party much impressed by sight of the other. At the suggestion of Deerfoot, Victor Shelton acted as spokesman.

"Helloa!" called the lad, "Who are you?"

A man answered in a clear voice:

"This is a United States expedition under Captains Lewis and Clark, on its way to the Pacific Ocean. Who are you?"

"This is an American expedition under Deerfoot the Shawanoe, on its way from the Pacific Ocean."

The man turned and said something to a companion near him. They seemed amused by the reply, and the former speaker called back:

"Won't you join us in camp?"

"We shall be glad to do so. We are hunting for a ford."

"I don't think you will find any. We will send our canoes to you and you can swim your horses over."

"We shall be very much obliged, and shall be glad to stay with you till morning."

A few minutes later two canoes, each in charge of a single man, put out from the southern shore and were paddled across the Missouri to our friends. The luggage was removed from the back of Zigzag and placed in one of the boats, which was so deeply laden that it could carry no one beside the white man. The other was buoyant enough, though severely taxed, to sustain the four. The horses swam beside the boats.

When Deerfoot took his place he said to the white man:

"My brother has worked hard. Will he not let Deerfoot take the paddle?"

"I have no objection," replied the other, with a grin, "if you think you know how to do it better than I."

"No better than my brother, but I hope nearly as well."

"Just watch him," added Victor. "If there's anybody on either side of the Mississippi that can beat that Shawanoe handling a canoe, I'll eat him, boots and all."

Deerfoot had no wish to display his skill, but since it was impossible for him to paddle without doing that he quickly won the admiration of the fellow, who was tired and glad to be relieved from work. He noted the easy grace and slight effort with which the dusky youth drove the craft athwart the current, quickly leaving the other boat behind, and called to his companion:

"Pete, he knows his business! Never seen his like. Hitch your canoe fast and he'll tow you over without using more than one hand and with both eyes shet."

Deerfoot acted as if he did not understand the words, and impelled the craft so accurately that when it touched shore it did so at a point precisely opposite the spot where he and his companions had entered the craft.

While our friends were crossing the Missouri the explorers completed their preparations for the evening. They had toiled hard all day in pulling, pushing and paddling the boats up stream, for there were not many places where progress could be made by any other means. The pirogues were furnished with sails, and now and then a strong favorable wind lightened the toil of the men.

When Deerfoot and the boys stepped out of the boat and came up the low but steep bank, two persons, attired in rough garb resembling that worn by hunters, came forward and cordially received them. The one in advance extended his hand and said:

"I am Captain Meriwether Lewis, and this is my friend, Captain William Clark. We are glad to meet you."

As he spoke he offered his hand to George Shelton, who introduced himself and then his companions.

"This is my twin brother Victor, though he hardly looks it. This is our guide, Deerfoot the Shawanoe."

The two officers welcomed the little party, and Captain Lewis added:

"We should be glad to have you spend several days with us, but you seem to be traveling in the opposite direction."

"Yes," said George, "we are homeward bound, and have been gone so long that we feel in somewhat of a hurry."

"May I ask where your home is?"

"In southern Ohio, at the settlement of Woodvale, near the mouth of the Miami."

"You are a long way from there."

"Yes," Victor took it upon himself to remark, "but we have been a good deal farther."

"When did you leave Woodvale?"

"About a year ago."

"And how far west have you been?"

"Far enough to get a glimpse of the Pacific Ocean."

"That is *our* destination. We thought we were to be the first white men to make the journey."

"So you will be, for we did not go all the way to the coast. I suppose you will do that?"

"Such are our instructions from President Jefferson."

While this conversation was going on other members of the exploring party gathered round. George had yielded the place of spokesman to his brother, and Deerfoot stood a few paces behind him. He was conscious of the curious scrutiny he was under from several of the members, but he acted as if unaware of it and held his peace. But he, too, was using his eyes and listening to the talk of the leaders, in whom he was much interested.

Victor fancied he detected just a shade of disappointment in the last remark of Captain Lewis, and he hastened to add:

"We amount to nothing. Only two of us belong to your race, and we cannot ask to be considered as men for a few years to come."

"You are husky-looking youngsters," added Captain Clark, from his place beside his associate, as he looked admiringly at the two lads.

"Where did you spend the winter?" continued Lewis.

"In the Blackfoot country, to the northwest. We reached there last autumn and stayed until a few weeks ago."

"I need not ask you if you were well treated, for your looks show that."

"They were all our friends. We should have perished so far north had we not found refuge among them."

"But we are forgetting our hospitality. We will have your horses looked after. Come over by the camp for supper, which will soon be ready. That is the finest horse I ever saw. Which of you is his owner?"

"He belongs to Deerfoot."

"Where did he get him?"

"Last year the Shawanoe's horse was hurt so badly that he had to kill him. Soon after we came across this stallion and Deerfoot managed to capture and tame him."

"He looks as if he might have been the king of a drove."

"He was. The Shawanoe cut him out and conquered him."

Now Deerfoot, while crossing the river, had warned the boys not to indulge in any boasts about him, as you know they were fond of doing. Despite his matchless prowess and skill, he disliked, above everything else, to be paraded before others and to be forced into showing what he was able to do. It was painful to George and Victor to be compelled to suppress their feelings in this way, but they meant to obey their friend, so far as they possibly could.

It was evident that neither Captain Lewis nor Clark nor any of the listeners believed the statement just made by Victor Shelton. The latter glanced at the Shawanoe for permission to explain. Deerfoot wrinkled his brow and shook his head. So the explanation was not made—just then.

The group now sauntered over to the large fire that had been kindled a few rods back from the river bank. Three men were busy preparing the evening meal, the others sauntering here and there, looking after the luggage, a portion of which had been brought ashore. Deerfoot walked over to Whirlwind, who was expecting such attention, and guided him some distance inland, where there was plenty of succulent grass and he could graze apart from the common herd. That equine would never lose his pride until he died. Patting his nose and softly bidding him good-bye, the Shawanoe hastened back to his friends, who had seated themselves on a fallen tree on one side of the fire, while Captains Lewis and Clark were similarly placed opposite. Two of the men were passing around ordinary tin plates, but no knives and no forks were called into use, one's fingers serving in their stead.

A Visit from Captains Lewis and Clark.

The explorers had not suffered from any lack of game. The catfish taken from the river weighed three or four pounds apiece, and several deer, elks and bears had been shot. Among the latter was one belonging to the grizzly species. To show the tenacity of these mammoth brutes, the journal of the explorers records that after the beast had been shot through the heart "he ran at his usual pace nearly a quarter of a mile before he fell." Wild geese were seen in such numbers that their killing often became so easy that it could not be called sport.

By the time our friends had completed their meal night had fully come, and the drop in the temperature made the warmth of the blaze pleasant. A second fire had been started at some distance, where most of the men gathered. Being apart from their leaders, there was more freedom of action and speech. In the course of the evening the boys heard the strains of a violin coming from the other camp, and, turning their heads, saw one of the men seated on a boulder with his head thrown back and vigorously sawing on his fiddle, while his companions were dancing in the open space in front, which was lit up by the firelight. Most of the hardy fellows solemnly swayed their bodies and shuffled back and forth with their arms akimbo, but others were more lively and dashed off jigs, reels and rigadoons. A French *voyageur* suddenly threw up his heels, supporting himself on his hands, and kept excellent time to the notes of the fiddle.

Neither Lewis nor Clark had ever heard of Deerfoot, but it soon developed that three of their men, Joseph and Reuben Shields and George Shannon, of Kentucky, knew a good deal about him. Shannon was but a boy himself, being only seventeen years old, but had once met the Shawanoe along the Ohio, when he was in the company of Simon Kenton. Deerfoot recalled the incident, and was glad to renew the acquaintance. At the invitation of Shannon he walked with him to the farther camp fire, and became a pleased witness of the boisterous sport of the men.

CHAPTER XXIII.
LEWIS AND CLARK'S EXPEDITION.

With George and Victor Shelton seated on the fallen tree on one side of the camp fire, and Captains Lewis and Clark on the other, these two famous explorers told the story of their expedition, which must always retain an historical interest for all of us.

As early as 1785, while Jefferson was in Paris, he became impressed with the value of the Northwest. This interest increased after his return home, and when he became President he secured an appropriation of twenty-five hundred dollars from Congress for the purpose of defraying the expense of an exploration of the vast region to the northwest of the Mississippi. This appropriation was made in February, 1803.

The area of Louisiana was more than a million square miles, and greater than that of the whole United States as it then existed. It was purchased from France for the sum of fifteen million dollars, the treaty to that effect between the two governments being ratified in the summer of the year named. By this single transaction the dominion of the United States was extended across the whole continent of North America, from the Atlantic to the Pacific.

The exploring party that entered this enormous region was under the command of Captains Meriwether Lewis and William Clark. It will be noted that both of these officers held the same rank. Military law does not permit the anomaly of equal authority, and Clark was really the junior, but in point of fact the rights of the two were the same. They were so considerate toward each other that no difference ever arose, and "the actual command and conduct of the expedition devolved upon each in exactly equal degree."

Lewis belonged to an old Virginia family and early displayed enterprise, boldness and discretion. He won the promotion to a captaincy at the age of twenty-two, and was barely thirty years of age when called to take part in this memorable exploration. Clark was also a native of Virginia, but his childhood had been spent in Kentucky, whither his parents removed. He was a younger brother of the more famous General George Rogers Clark, but for whom the

Allegheny Mountains instead of the Mississippi would have been our western boundary after the close of the Revolution. He was about thirty-three years old when he joined Lewis. He possessed excellent qualities, and it may be said that no two persons could have been selected who were better fitted to lead the score and a half of men across the continent.

On July 5, 1803, Captain Lewis left Washington, hoping to gather his men and materials in time to reach La Charrette, the upper white settlement on the Missouri, and there spend the winter. The inevitable delays followed, and the Spanish commandant of the province, not having received official notice of the transfer, would not allow the expedition to pass through the territory. The explorers, therefore, went into camp for the winter at the mouth of the Du Bois River, a little north of St. Louis, on the eastern bank of the Mississippi. This point was left on May 14, 1804. Entering the Indian country the leaders held a council with the Ottoes and Missouris, and by the distribution of gewgaws and presents won the good will of the red men. Lewis and Clark named the place of meeting Council Bluff, which is retained to this day, although the site of the modern city is below the meeting place and on the opposite, side of the river.

For a time the expedition acted the part of peacemaker among the Indians. The officers patched up peace agreements between the tribes that were on the verge of warfare, and made treaties with the Yankton branch of the Sioux and the Ricaras. All these natives were familiar with white men, having known both French traders and the employees of the British Fur Company. The Indians showed a friendly disposition toward the explorers, but their wonder was unbounded at sight of the African servant, he being the first of his race they had ever seen. With the waggery of his nature this negro gravely informed them that he was really a wild animal that had been caught and tamed. The simple folk believed his fantastic yarns, which were emphasized by numerous feats of strength on his part.

Progress up the river was slow, because of the many sand bars and numerous curves of the stream. The hunters, who kept in advance, secured large quantities of fresh meat, and dried a good deal for the winter supply. The region of the Mandans was reached in the latter part of October. There a fort was built and occupied during the winter. This was in what is now McLean County, North Dakota. The winter was very severe, and many of the men had their hands and feet frostbitten, while the continual glare of the snow caused a temporary blindness.

At this fort another interpreter was engaged. He was a Canadian, whose wife was a member of the Snake tribe of Indians of the Rocky Mountains. She was stolen when a child and brought east, where she was bought by the Canadian, who made her his wife. She was a remarkable woman, and the only one of her sex who accompanied the party. When she set out she carried an infant barely two months old. She not only stood the journey as well as any of the men, but displayed a rare degree of intelligence. She remembered much of the wild region through which the party had to pass, and smoothed the way among her own race for the white invaders. She became very popular with all the members, and deserved the praise which the leaders gave her.

Six canoes were soon completed. The company made their start April 7, 1805, sixteen going down stream with a barge laden with curiosities of the region for President Jefferson, while thirty-two formed the permanent party, which pressed into the great unknown region spreading out before them. The names of all these explorers are preserved in the archives of the War Department under the title of "A roll of the men who accompanied Captains Lewis and Clark on their late tour to the Pacific Ocean through the interior of the continent of North America, showing their rank, with some remarks on their respective merits and services."

Early as was the season, the men suffered much from mosquitoes. Spring kept company with the expedition. Herds of deer, elk, buffaloes and antelopes were seen grazing on the rich grass, and there seemed no end to swans and geese. Passing the alkali regions, the party reached, in the latter part of April, the mouth of a large river, to which they gave the name of Yellowstone. Joseph Fields, of Kentucky, ascended it for eight miles, and was the first white man to do so. Rains, high winds and cold weather welcomed them into the hills of Montana, and often the boats had to be dragged along the banks by means of elk-skin cords. They were thus laboriously making their way when, as has been shown, they were met by Deerfoot and the Shelton brothers at the mouth of the Musselshell River.

The story of the Lewis and Clark expedition, therefore, ended for George and Victor Shelton at the point named. It will not be uninteresting, however, to sum up the history of one of the most memorable enterprises connected with the development of the West. Captains Lewis and Clark gained a great deal of valuable knowledge from the boys, who had traversed a large part of the region which they intended to explore. The excellent memories and the marked intelligence of the youths were admired by the officers.

A few days after the meeting between the two parties Lewis climbed to the top of the highest elevation north of the river and gained his first view of the Rocky Mountains, known at that time as the Stony Mountains. All the numerous streams were described and named. It has been charged against the explorers that they were lacking in sentiment and imagination, for most of the names thus given by them have been supplanted by others, but it cannot be said that these changes have always been an improvement.

On the second day of summer the explorers had to face a puzzling problem. A large branch flowing from the north was so similar to the Missouri that it seemed it must be that river, while the one hitherto accepted as such bore to the south. Which was the branch that, according to the reports of the Indians, had its rise in the Rocky Mountains, near the source of the Columbia? To settle the question the party divided, one ascending either branch. Upon reuniting it was agreed that the south branch was the real Missouri. The northern stream was named the Maria. This was another of the few instances in which the title given by the explorers stuck.

The rapids five miles below the Falls of the Missouri were reached on June 15. These had to be passed by a portage. An idea can be formed of the great difficulties encountered when it is stated that, although the portage was hardly eighteen miles long, it took eleven days to make it. The men, however, were in high spirits, and at night Peter Cruzatte added to the "gayety of nations" by playing on his violin.

About the middle of August horses were obtained from the tribe from which the Indian wife of the interpreter had been stolen. The passage through the mountains or over the Divide caused the greatest suffering of the expedition. The men had to cut their way in many places through the brush, clamber over jagged stones and climb such precipitous walls that several of their horses were crippled. Then snow began falling and the nights became very cold. Game seemed to have deserted the country, and the sufferers had to eat all their supply of flour and parched corn. Beginning with September 14, they were obliged to kill and eat some of their horses, and even at that had to be very sparing or the supply would have been exhausted.

Descending the western side of the mountains, however, they found abundant edible roots, dried salmon and dried berries at the Indian villages. The famishing men feasted so ravenously that most of them became ill. New canoes were constructed, and leaving their horses with a chief they started down the Clearwater and reached the Columbia on October 16. Ten days were occupied in making the portage of the falls and rapids, and on the morning of November 7, when the fog lifted, they saw in the distance the Pacific Ocean.

A month later the party went into winter quarters. It rained eternally, the weather was chilly and their condition for a long time was miserable in the extreme. The shelter built for themselves was called Fort Clatsop. There they remained until March 23, 1806, when the explorers set out on their return journey. They had to face difficulties, hardships and sufferings again, but they had learned from experience and were better prepared to do so. They embarked on the Yellowstone July 24, and ten days later reached its junction with the Missouri. At this point the men were driven almost frantic by the mosquitoes. At midday, September 23, 1806, they arrived at St. Louis, where the whole town turned out to welcome them. There the party was disbanded, and, passing to their various destinations, the Lewis and Clark expedition took its place in history.

During the latter part of the chat between Lewis and Clark, Deerfoot came quietly forward and sat down beside the Shelton boys. He listened closely to all that was said. When the officers asked questions, the Shawanoe left the answers to the brothers. But more than once they were in doubt, and turned to him for aid. His prompt response in every instance was noticed by the officers, who, after a time, addressed their questions almost wholly to him.

Finally, at a late hour, the visitors wrapped themselves in their blankets and stretched out on the ground, with their feet turned toward the blaze. The explorers always maintained a watch, for though they felt no fear of the Indians they were subject to unpleasant visits, as in the case when a bison swam a river and went plunging like a steam engine through the camp. Moreover, the men had seen enough of the grizzly bear to hold him in respectful awe, and they did not intend to have any of the brutes steal a march upon them.

The morning was clear and pleasant, and the explorers were astir at an early hour. A breakfast was made from catfish and goose, and a cordial farewell took place. The boys wished Captains Lewis and Clark the best of fortune, and Lewis complimented them, and especially Deerfoot, for the information they had given him of the region through which they expected to force their way. In return, Lewis advised his guests to bear directly to the south and not to follow the course of the Missouri, as he and his company had done. In fact, it would have been absurd for the three to adopt any other plan. They could make no use of the current because they had no boats, and if they procured them from the Indians they could not be made to carry the horses. The distance was much greater by the Lewis and Clark route, which held no attractions to our friends. When, therefore, Victor Shelton told Captain Lewis that his advice would be followed, he said that which had been determined upon before the meeting of the two parties.

CHAPTER XXIV.
OVERBOARD.

Our friends, after parting with the Lewis and Clark expedition, pressed southward, in search of a milder climate and a more direct route to their homes. They were traversing a region broken by many streams, detached mountain spurs and ranges of lofty elevation. Black Butte, as it is known to-day, in Dawson County, Montana, was left on the left, after which they rode through the valley of Little Porcupine Creek to the Yellowstone, which was crossed with considerable difficulty. Turning more to the east, they passed the rough, precipitous section, the scene many years afterward of the appalling Custer massacre, and now an immense Indian reservation, and, entering the present State of Wyoming, skirted the foothills of the well-known Big Horn range. Here the scenery was of the grandest character. Had the party not been accustomed for months to such impressive exhibitions of the majesty of nature, they could have spent weeks of enjoyment where the like is found in few parts of the world. They pushed on, however, not making what might be termed a real halt until they came to the Laramie Mountains, almost the equal of the former in picturesque beauty.

By this time the unremitting hard work began to tell upon the horses. Zigzag showed slight lameness, and Jack, the animal ridden by George Shelton, surely needed rest. Only Whirlwind continued as powerful, active and fresh as ever. Deerfoot and the boys always walked a number of miles each day, not only for the sake of the horses, but to gain the exercise each needed. Deerfoot ran races with Whirlwind, who was inconsiderate enough to beat him every time. Sometimes they frolicked like a couple of boys. The Shawanoe delighted to tease the noble creature, who delighted to have him do so. One habit of the youth was to pretend he was offended with the stallion. He would turn his back upon him and repel his advances toward a reconciliation. Whirlwind would poke his nose first over one shoulder and then the other, rubbing it against the cheek of Deerfoot. If the latter sulked too long, Whirlwind would show his impatience by flirting his head against that of the youth, whirling about, kicking up his heels and galloping off. No words could have said more plainly:

"I don't care. Pout all you want to. I shan't coax you any more. I haven't much opinion of you anyway."

And then Deerfoot had to make peace with his offended majesty. But the stallion never held off long, and George and Victor laughed at the antics of the couple.

The halt of which I have spoken was made one afternoon, near the southern end of the Laramie range. No more favorable spot could have been selected, for the grass was abundant and of the best quality. A stream of considerable size issued from the mountains and flowing northeast joined the North Platte, a hundred miles away, and there was enough timber to yield all the fuel needed. The horses were unsaddled and unbridled, the pack removed from the back of Zigzag and the three owners were at liberty to do whatever they chose to pass away the hours. It was so late that they stayed in camp till morning, when it was decided to set off on a hunt, Deerfoot going by himself, while the brothers, as usual, kept company.

There had hardly been a day since parting from Lewis and Clark that our friends had not seen Indians or signs of them. Sometimes it was the smoke of their camp fires in the distance, and then they caught sight of a band of horsemen, who might number three or four or five times as many warriors. It was the rule of Deerfoot to avoid coming in contact with these wanderers, so long as he could do so without rousing their suspicion by his actions. While in a general way the strangers could be counted upon as friendly, they contained a ratio of lawless if not desperate characters, who were liable to be tempted by the hope of plunder. Whirlwind was quite sure to attract envious eyes. Moreover, the party was now in a region which was visited, more or less, by trappers and hunters in the employ of fur companies, or who operated independently. The majority of these men were rough and reckless of the rights of others. They had little faith in the Golden Rule where Indians were concerned, and affrays between them and the native inhabitants were numerous. Many a white man who went into the mountains never came out again. He fell a victim to his own wrongdoing and received the fate he had invited so long. Others succeeded in getting through the lines with their pack animals laden with peltries, to St. Louis, to return again the following autumn and to face and overcome, or possibly fail to overcome, the perils they had met so often.

The sun was shining from a clear, balmy sky, for summer had come, when Deerfoot swept every portion of the visible horizon with the spyglass without detecting a sign of red men. To the westward towered the immense Laramie range, while the plains stretched eastward and were crossed by numerous streams, on whose banks thriving towns and cities have been built in later days. Less than a hundred miles to the southeast was the site of the present city of Cheyenne.

Before reaching the scene of this encampment the travelers had twice come within range of grizzly bears. The first was ignored, but the second did not choose to be passed by in such cavalier fashion. He first appeared close to camp, much to the terror of the horses, and then deliberately proceeded to attack everything in sight. He came within a hair, too, of killing Zigzag and Prince before he was brought low by the bullets of all three, Deerfoot burying two in the colossal carcass.

Black and cinnamon bears were observed, but no disturbance followed on the part of men or brutes. Several times the wolves, coyotes and pumas became so troublesome that a number were killed. Bison were so plentiful that hardly a day passed without sight of them. In some instances the droves contained tens of thousands.

George and Victor Shelton soon found themselves climbing among the foothills. Deerfoot had gone in another direction, the agreement being that they should return to camp soon after meridian, and not to go far from headquarters. While none felt misgiving as to danger, all had learned to be circumspect.

It may be said that the stroll of the boys was as much to gain exercise as to hunt game, though the latter object was the one avowed by them. In those days a person did not have to look far for such sport, but it seemed as if the wild animals scented the danger and kept out of the way. When noon came the tired boys sat down beside a mountain torrent, without either having fired his rifle.

"We haven't heard the report of Deerfoot's gun," said George, "and I don't see that there is any use of hunting further."

"Nor do I. I'm hungry and we shan't be able to get anything to eat this side of camp. It must be the game noticed that *I* was with you, and they have all run to their holes."

"We have one consolation," remarked George, ignoring the last sentence. "It will be easier getting back to camp, for it's down hill all the way."

"But we shall have a good deal of climbing to do. I'm ready to say I've gained enough exercise to last me till to-morrow. I think," added Victor, rising to his feet and looking at the noisy torrent a few feet in front, "that we can shorten the distance by crossing that."

"How are we going to do it? We're not likely to find it bridged."

"I'm sure we shall be able to leap across."

The two walked to the edge of the stream, which may be described as a furious torrent, rushing between the rocks, which were separated by a dozen feet, the upper margin being one or two feet above the surface of the stream. Standing on the edge of the small cañon and looking down, the boys saw that the water was of crystalline clearness and was beaten in many places into froth and foam, which sparkled with every color of the rainbow as it shot into the sunlight. The course of the torrent was so tortuous and the turns so abrupt that clouds of mist curled upward in places and caused the rocks to drip with moisture. The roar was so loud that the brothers had to shout to each other.

"We might make a running leap here," said George, "but it isn't worth while to take the risk."

"There must be narrower portions. Let's look."

Turning to the left, they had to go only a little way when they found a favorable place. The breadth was no more than seven or eight feet. While they could not shorten the distance to camp very much, the advantage was worth striving for.

"No risk in that," remarked Victor, looking at his brother, who nodded his head to signify he agreed with him.

"I'll jump first," added Victor, walking back several paces to gain the necessary start. He could have made the leap without this preparation, but was using only ordinary prudence. George stood to one side and close to the edge, so as to observe every phase of the performance. Despite the apparent safety of the attempt, a strange misgiving came over George, and he turned to his brother to protest, when he saw he had started on his brief run. He carried his rifle in his right hand, took a number of short steps, measuring the distance with his eye, so that the take-off should be exact, and covered the space in a second or two.

George was watching every movement of the supple limbs, when he uttered an exclamation of horror. At the very moment Victor was gathering his muscles for the leap, and when close to the edge, the dripping stone caused his foot to slip. He fell sideways, let go of his rifle, which shot over the edge, and desperately struggled to check himself. Had there been five seconds at command he would have been saved. George, who made the attempt, could have dashed forward and grasped a foot or leg. Victor could have stopped, but the rock on which he had fallen seemed to be covered with plumbago. While frantically clutching and vainly trying to grasp some obstruction that would overcome his momentum, he slid over the edge and dropped into the boiling cauldron below. The accident was begun and finished, as may be said, in the twinkling of an eye.

Wild with affright, George ran to the edge of the torrent and peered over. He caught a glimpse of his brother a dozen yards away, spinning down the torrent. He saw his head for a moment, and then his arms thrown upward, as he disappeared, blindly but vainly struggling to save himself. In an instant he was whirled round a bend in the cañon, his body flung aloft by the resistless force of the torrent, but hurled hither and thither, as helpless as a log of wood.

Frantic and hardly conscious of what he was doing, George dashed along the edge of the cañon, which sped faster than he could run. One moment he was on the point of leaping into the raging waters in the blind effort to save Victor, but the certainty that that would only add another victim held him in restraint, and he continued running, stumbling and praying in agony for Heaven to intercede while it was yet time.

Suddenly he saw a man standing on the other side of the cañon some rods below, and staring wonderingly at him. George raised his voice so that it pierced the uproar like the notes of a trumpet:

"Save him! Save him! He fell into the water!"

CHAPTER XXV.
JACK HALLOWAY AGAIN.

The man was quick-witted. The words and the frenzied gestures told a story which he understood. Standing close to the edge of the stream, he peered into it and caught sight of a white face, loosely flapping limbs and the helpless drift of a human being, borne toward him with the speed of a race horse. The top of the bank was so near the surface that the man dropped on his face, so as to be able to reach forward and downward to the foaming torrent.

He saw the body coming, and braced himself for the herculean effort that would be necessary in the next breath. Reaching so far that he was in danger of losing his own balance, he coolly awaited the critical moment. Then his big hand closed like the paw of a grizzly bear on the shoulder of Victor Shelton. A tremendous wrench and he was dragged out and dropped limp and senseless at the feet of his rescuer.

George Shelton saw this much, and, hardly knowing what he was doing, made a desperate effort to leap the chasm, that he might join the couple. But his foot slipped, too, and only by a superhuman effort did he save himself from tumbling into the swirling wrath of water. Scrambling to his feet, he sped downward to Victor and the stranger. The latter showed his coolness by getting to work without the least delay. Victor was senseless and had swallowed a good deal of water. He seemed to be drowned.

The man held him by the heels and was standing him on his head. Then he rolled him over and pressed his chest, with that oscillation which is helpful in restoring seemingly drowned persons, while the breathless George stood idly by watching everything with straining eyes. He could do nothing but pray and hope.

At the end of a minute or two he saw, with joy unspeakable, the signs of returning life. Victor was on his back, as if dead, when he partly opened his eyes; but there was no expression in them. His rescuer was scrutinizing the lad's face and noted the awakening of consciousness. Straightening up, he said with a sigh:

"He's all right now; but he couldn't have come nigher pegging out."

"You have saved him! You have saved him! Oh, how can I thank you?"

And yielding to the reaction, George sobbed like a child. The stranger looked at him without speaking, and gave his attention again to the prostrate form. Victor speedily regained his senses, and, with a little help from the man, sat up. He stared wonderingly at his new friend and then at his brother, striving manfully to master his emotions. With the waggery that cropped up at the most unexpected times, he turned to George with the question:

"Are you crying because he saved my life?"

"I'm crying for joy. I had given up all hope."

"So had I. I tell you I came pretty near being a goner. Please help me up."

George took his hand and almost lifted Victor to his feet. As he came up he made a grimace, because of the pain that wrenched him. He was so battered and bruised that the wonder was that several bones had not been broken.

"Where's my rifle?" suddenly asked Victor, looking about him.

"In the bottom of the cañon, I reckon."

"Mebbe you'd like to make a dive for it," suggested the man.

"No, I've had enough of that. How shall I thank you for what you have done?"

"By not saying anything about it. By a piece of good luck I happened to be on the spot in time to give you a lift."

The boys now looked more closely at the Good Samaritan. He was attired in the dress common among the trappers and hunters of the Northwest in those days, and was a magnificent specimen of physical manhood, being fully six feet in height, with a broad, massive frame and an immense grizzled beard, which flowed over his chest and covered his face almost to the eyes. He had laid down his long, formidable rifle when he hurried to the rescue of the boy, and he now stooped and picked up the weapon. Moving back a few paces, so as to get beyond the noise made by the rushing waters, he said, in his gruff but not unpleasant voice:

"Tell me how this thing happened."

George briefly gave the particulars of the mishap, to which the man silently listened.

"You ain't the only younker or man either who has lost all by a little slip. The next time you want to make a big jump be sure of your footing. What are you two chaps doing in this part of the world?"

"We have been across the continent, almost to the Pacific, and are now on the way to our home in Ohio."

"You ain't traveling alone, are you?"

"No; we have a companion, who is off somewhere in the mountains, but will soon join us in camp."

"'Pears to me you've been on a powerful long tramp."

"We have. We spent last winter among the Blackfeet, and are homesick."

"I reckon your camp ain't fur off, and we may as well go there."

"We shall be glad to have you with us, for you have proved the best of friends."

"Thar! Thar! Drop that; talk about something else."

When Victor tried to walk he had to lean on the shoulder of his brother, and the pain from his bruises compelled him at times to stop and rest. The burly trapper offered to help, but Victor thanked him and got on quite well with the assistance of George. The man walked a few paces behind the two, that he might not hurry them too much, and because it belonged to the boys to act as guide.

"Who is the man you've got with you?"

"He is a young Shawanoe Indian named Deerfoot," replied George Shelton.

"What!" exclaimed the trapper, stopping as if shot. "Do you mean that handsome young warrior who went through the country below us last summer with a Blackfoot redskin and two younkers?"

"The same. We are the boys that were with him."

"Wal, I'll be skulped!" added the other, as if he could not do justice to his feelings. "I never dreamed of anything like *that*."

"Like what?" asked George.

"Seeing that Shawanoe agin. Say, he's a great one, ain't he?"

"You know him, then?"

"Wal, I reckon. He done me the greatest favor of my life—greater than what I done that chap of yourn a little while ago."

"I don't see how that can be," remarked the limping Victor; "but Deerfoot is always doing good to others."

"Didn't he ever tell you anything about me?"

"You haven't told us your name."

"I'm Jack Halloway."

The boys agreed that they had never heard the Shawanoe mention him by name. Victor added:

"He is the last one to speak of his good deeds, and he doesn't like to hear anyone else speak of them."

"He'll hear some one talk when I see him," chuckled the trapper, with a shaking of his herculean shoulders.

Because of Victor's hurts the descent among the foothills to camp took a long time, and the afternoon was well gone when the three reached headquarters. While a little way off the three caught sight of the Shawanoe, who had started a fire and was broiling buffalo steak for supper. He looked with surprise at the sight of Victor leaning on the shoulder of his brother and walking with difficulty, and at the towering form behind them. Ceasing his work, he came forward to greet the party. He paid no attention to the man until George Shelton told of the mishap in which the life of Victor was saved by the person behind them.

During this brief interchange the trapper kept in the background, with his eyes on the Shawanoe. Needless to say, Deerfoot had recognized him at the first glance. Not suspecting this, the man now came forward, the moving of the beard about his mouth showing that he was grinning and chuckling.

"I reckon you don't remember me, Deerfoot."

"Deerfoot could never forget his brother, Jack Halloway," replied the youth, extending his hand, which was warmly grasped by the trapper.

"I'm powerful glad to meet you agin, Shawanoe, though I hadn't much hope of ever doing so. Talk about friends, you beat 'em all, and I'll be skulped if you don't look handsomer than ever—no you don't, for that couldn't be. Shake agin, pardner."

Deerfoot was as pleased to meet his old acquaintance as the latter was to see him. All seated themselves on the ground about the blaze, and as night had not yet come the meal was deferred until more was learned of what had taken place during the interval between the former meeting and the present coming together.

"Why is my brother in the mountains at this season of the year?" asked Deerfoot, when the trapper had lit his pipe.

Of course cold weather is the time for trapping fur-bearing animals. The custom in the olden days was for the hunters to go into the mountains in the autumn, spend the time until spring in gathering peltries, and then bring them to civilization for sale. It was now summer, and it was not to be supposed that Jack Halloway was engaged on professional business in the Laramie Mountains. He explained:

"Last fall I took a partner—Dick Burley by name—and we put in the winter among the beaver runs and mountains over to the northwest. We done so poor that I let Dick start with the pack animals for St. Louis, without me going with him. He hadn't more than half a load, and we made up our minds that we'd got to find new trapping grounds or we shouldn't make enough to pay for our salt. So me and Dick parted and I've been on the tramp for two months."

"How did you make out?" asked Victor, who, having found an easy position for his aching body, felt it his duty to join in the discussion.

"I hit it when I came to this part of the country. A few miles south are hundreds of beaver, foxes, otter and other critters whose furs we're after. I don't think a single one of 'em has ever been trapped. There's where me and Dick will try it next fall."

"Then you will soon go home?"

"I intended to start to-morrow. My horse is a little way back among the foothills, stuffing himself with enough grass to last him a week."

"My brother will go with us," said the pleased Deerfoot.

"If you don't feel too proud to have me for company, I'll be mighty glad to go with you."

"Nothing will suit us better," said George, heartily. It was natural that he and Victor should feel profoundly grateful to the trapper. Even had he not done them so measureless a service they would have liked him from the first.

It was not until the night had fully come, the evening meal eaten and the fire replenished, though the weather remained mild, that a full interchange took place among the different members of the little party. Victor suffered less from his bruises, and with his blanket wrapped about his shoulders showed no effects from his terrifying adventure. The horses were left to themselves, Jack Halloway saying that no attention need be given to his, despite the possibility of some thieving Indian making off with him. The trapper expressed unbounded admiration of Whirlwind, and could not understand how Deerfoot had ever gained such a piece of property. George and Victor did not dare to explain in the presence of the Shawanoe, but each determined to do so on the first opportunity, despite the risk of another "disciplining" at the hands of the modest youth.

After Jack had smoked awhile and the chat had gone on without any special point, he turned to the Shawanoe and said:

"I've seen you stealing a look at me now and then and I know what you done it for."

"Yes, Deerfoot did so; but my brother cannot tell the reason."

"You've been trying to find out from my looks whether I've stuck to the pledge I made you a year ago to give up drinking whiskey."

"That was the reason; Deerfoot was almost but not quite certain."

"Have you any doubts left?"

The Shawanoe smiled.

"Only a shadow."

"Wal, you can kick that shadow out of sight! I haven't drank a drop of the stuff since that night, a year ago, when I flung my flask into the creek, after hearing your sermon, that shook me down to my toes."

Deerfoot leaned over and offered his hand again to happy Jack Halloway, who turned to the boys.

"Being as he never told you, I might as well give you the story."

Thereupon the trapper related in his characteristic fashion the incident of which you heard long ago. The eyes of the boys kindled and Victor said:

"That is only one of a hundred things Deerfoot has done."

Catching a warning look from the Shawanoe, Victor said in desperation:

"I'm not going to try to give a list, Deerfoot, but won't you let me tell Jack how you whipped the greatest war chief of the Blackfeet and how he became a Christian?"

"There is no need of that, but my brothers may tell what happened to them when they disobeyed Deerfoot."

"I'll do that if you don't shut down on the other story."

The Shawanoe would have refused, but the trapper's curiosity had been stirred and he insisted upon hearing of the incident. As a compromise the Indian youth rose to his feet and sauntered out to where Whirlwind was still cropping the juicy herbage. He would not stay and listen to what he knew was about to be said. The boys were glad to have him absent, for it left them free to speak what they pleased, and you may be sure that Victor and George did not mince matters. Their account of that remarkable combat and its results was told with graphic eloquence. Then George added the story of Deerfoot's encounter with the grizzly bear and his defeat of the Assiniboine, whose life he spared. Inasmuch as the boys had never been able to draw the particulars of that combat from Deerfoot, Victor had to embellish it with his own imagination, and he did it to perfection. He was in the midst of a description of how the Shawanoe beat the best marksmen, runners and leapers of the Blackfeet when Deerfoot came back to the camp fire.

"Now let my brothers tell of what happened to them when Deerfoot was through with Taggarak."

"You needn't worry; I didn't forget that. Well, Jack, you see Deerfoot forbade me and George to come anywhere near, but we couldn't stay away. He found it out, cut a big gad and splintered it over our shoulders and we couldn't help ourselves."

And then Jack Halloway threw back his head and roared with laughter, declaring that he had never heard so good a story.

CHAPTER XXVI.
A TEMPERANCE AGITATOR.

"I'll never forget that ride home last year," said Jack Halloway, "after I pulled out in the night and left Deerfoot with you younkers asleep by the camp fire. It took me a week to reach St. Louis, and there wasn't a drop of whiskey to be had on the road. For two or three days I was the most miserable critter that ever limped on two legs. I'd have give my whole load of peltries to get that flask back agin, but there was no help for it. Twice I rode up to the camp fires of Injins, hoping to buy some fire water from them, but neither party had a drop. Then I buckled down to it.

"On the fourth night when I camped I was almost crazy. As I rolled about in my blanket, not able to sleep a wink, I remembered what Deerfoot had said to me about praying. Strange I'd never thought of it before. Wal, I got on my knees, and if ever a poor wretch prayed it was Jack Halloway, and I kept it up for two or three hours. I was about ready to let go when *the thing which I was praying for came to me!*

"Just as plain as I have heard your voices, I catched the words, 'It's all right; you've conquered your temptation; you're boss now.' Some folks may laugh, but it won't do for 'em to say where Jack Halloway can hear 'em that thar's nothing in the Christian religion. I know better, 'cause I've got it right there!" exclaimed the trapper, thumping his heart.

"From that time forward everything was rosy with me. The sun never shone so bright, the birds never sung so sweet and I never felt so happy through and through. I shouted and yelled for joy and walloped the horses, just because I couldn't help it. If I had met anyone at those times he would have set me down as drunk. So I was—drunk with pure joy and religion.

"At St. Louis I sold my peltries for the biggest price I've got in ten years. I took the money home and throwed it into the lap of my little, sweet, gray-haired mother, who just stared at me, not knowing what it meant. When I made it all clear she began crying, and then she dropped on her knees and I dropped alongside of her, and when she got through praying I took up the job and kept things humming for another half hour. After I'd let up I grabbed her in my arms, and we danced about that cabin, just as she used to do when she was the belle of the town, and we laughed and frolicked and made a couple of fools of ourselves.

"When she asked me to tell her the meaning of my short rein-up and change of my life, I give her the whole thing. It was the work of a young Shawanoe Injin called Deerfoot, who was the most ginooine Christian on either side of the old Mississippi. She asked all about you, Deerfoot, and she said she hoped she would meet you some day. So when we get back to St. Louis I'll introduce you."

"Deerfoot will be glad to see the mother of my brother," softly replied the Shawanoe, in a voice tremulous with feeling. He and the boys listened with absorbed interest to the graphic story told by the trapper.

"French Pete keeps the worst whiskey hole along the Mississippi. It is down by the river side and is the main drinking place in the town. He has got hundreds of dollars from the families of the trappers who come down the river in the spring, and for years he has gathered in about every cent I could rake together.

"Wal, after I had been home about a week I strolled down to his place one moonlight night. I told mother not to worry about me, for I would blow my own head off before I'd ever swaller another drop of red p'ison. When I opened the door of the ramshackle cabin, Pete looked up with a grin, and said as how he was wondering where I'd kept myself so long, for he had heerd I'd got back and done unusual well. He was glad to welcome me, and asked what I'd have and the treat was on him for old friendship's sake.

"There didn't happen to be anybody else in the place at the time, for it was early in the evening. I walked up to the bar and leaned on it familiar like, and asked Pete if he didn't think he'd made enough money in ruining other folks to quit the bus'ness. He showed he didn't know what I meant by the strange question. I then said I'd stopped the foolery for good, and give him my opinion of him as the worst wretch in town. He had sot out the whiskey bottle on the bar and shoved out the cork with his thumb and forefinger. I 'spose that was to let me get a whiff of the stuff. I got it. I reached out my hand, pushed the cork back in the bottle, and then grabbing it by the neck brought it down on the bar with a bang that broke it into a dozen pieces and sent the whiskey flying about the room.

"When Pete seed what I was up to he made a swipe at me, remarking several swear words at the same time, but I landed him one under the ear that sent him back so hard aginst the bottles behind him that he bounced forward agin, and I grabbed him.

"He made just the sort of club I wanted. You see I had him by the shoulders and I could swing his heels free and easy like. Wal, I used him that way. For the next ten or fifteen minutes the only music in that place was the panting of Pete and the crash and smash of bottles. The fumes of the stuff filled the room like the mist you sometimes see rising from a kenyon in the mountains. When I got through I don't believe there was a whole bottle left, and as I stepped about the floor I splashed in whiskey, just as we do when the Mississippi overflows the streets. I tossed Pete over into one corner, and, not seeing any more blessed work to do, passed out the door. I met two friends on their way for a drink. When they said good evening I remarked off-hand that they'd find plenty of whiskey inside without asking for it, and went on to my home.

"I expected Pete would make a row about what I'd done and I would be catched in the biggest kind of a row, but there ain't much law in St. Louis just now, on account of the change from Spanish rule to French and then to American. Besides, Pete hasn't got many friends, and I reckon he knew he wouldn't get much sympathy. He rigged up his place after awhile and laid in a new stock of p'ison, but it'll take a long time for him to make up the losses that follered his inviting Jack Halloway to have a drink. Shawanoe," added the trapper, abruptly turning to the Indian, "I want to ask you a question."

"Deerfoot will be glad to answer if he can."

"When I went down to French Pete's place and smashed things and cleaned it out, as I've been stating, did I do right?"

Instead of directly answering, the Shawanoe asked:

"Has the conscience of my brother ever whispered to him that he did wrong in breaking the whiskey bottles?"

"No, I rather think it's the other way. When I started home I felt my conscience clapping me on the shoulder and saying, 'You hit it right that time, old fellow,' and ever since, when I think of it, I hear the same soft words."

There was a twinkle in the eyes of Deerfoot as he gently replied:

"My brother should always do what his conscience tells him to do."

"Good! That settles it! But I've got something more interesting than all that to tell you. If French Pete didn't do anything to me for what I'd done to him, he laid a deep plan to get his revenge. You see he's afraid to tackle me in the open, for I may say there ain't a man living that Jack Halloway is afeard of—barring one."

"Who is he?" asked Victor Shelton, slyly nudging his brother.

"Deerfoot the Shawanoe."

The face of the Indian flushed and he protested:

"Deerfoot would be only a pappoose in the hands of my brother."

"P'raps, but you'd never be in his hands. I've studied your build and quickness, and the chap that can whip a Blackfoot war chief without using a weapon is the best fellow in the world to let alone—I beg pardon, Deerfoot. I'll drop it.

"When it was getting time for me to think about going to the beaver runs agin Dick Burley come to me and proposed that we should be pardners. Dick is a good fellow and I always liked him, for he hasn't a streak of yaller in his make-up. The only objection to him was that he liked firewater too well. He spent enough money at French Pete's to support that rogue. Dick's wife and two children were in rags, and the poor woman had to work herself almost to death to keep from starving. I had talked with Dick many times, not neglecting to give him a good cussing now and then, but it didn't amount to nothing. In the hope of being able to do him good I agreed to go with him to the Northwest.

"Wal, you wouldn't 'spicion what a trick French Pete and Dick was trying to play on me. It was the idea of Pete, but Dick promised to do his part. Pete agreed to let Dick have a whole keg of his best—or rather worst—whiskey without charging him a cent. He was to take it with us, with the sole purpose of getting me into the habit of drinking again. Their ca'clation was that when we got away up in the Northwest, where it was sometimes cold enough to freeze the tail off a brass monkey, and Dick took his swigs reg'lar like, I'd be sure to knock under and jine him. I couldn't stand it to see him enj'ying such bliss and telling what a lot of good it done him.

"I never spicioned anything of the kind, but when I set eyes on that keg stored among the things on our pack horses I fixed *my* plan of campaign. Being as it was meant to last four or five months-it wouldn't do for Dick to draw on it too heavy at the start. Then, too, as I said, he expected me to come in on the chorus, and he was saving up for that glad day.

"Every time Dick took a drink, which I must say waren't often, of course he invited me to jine, but when I said no, that was enough and he let me alone. Oh, he was shrewd, and was playing his cards like a boss of the game.

"Wal, we had only one brush with the Injins, and we got to the place we had fixed on without any harm, and with most of the whiskey still in the keg. It was where I had been doing my trapping for several years before I went further South, which was the reason I happened to meet you in that part of the world last summer.

"We set our traps as usual, turned our horses out to grass and stowed our blankets and things in a big holler tree, in which I had cut a door, with a buffalo skin that hung down in front. The first thing Dick carried in was the whiskey keg. 'I think more of that,' he remarked, as he sot it down tender like, as if it was a sick baby, 'than everything else in the outfit.' I made no reply, but I was busy thinking, and when he wa'nt looking I done some chuckling and laughing that would have made him open his eyes had he knowed of it.

"One night when Dick was sleeping particular sound I sneaked out of the holler tree with the keg. I had to be powerful careful, for we folks larn to sleep light, but I managed it without waking him. Having made up my mind long before what I would do, I didn't make any mistake. Raising the cask, with the stuff jingling and sploshing about inside, I brought it down on the p'int of a rock with a force that made it split open like a watermelon. In a few minutes every drop had soaked into the ground and it was a thousand miles to French Pete in St. Louis.

"I had to tell Dick the truth the next morning. The minute he opened his eyes he went for his morning dram. I remarked that we didn't need whiskey in them parts, and being as I had become a temperance man it was agin my principles to have any of the p'ison around.

"Wal, Dick was that mad he turned white. When he realized that there was no way of his getting a drink for months he collapsed. Then he roused up and said as how the insult, being a mortal one, we'd have to settle it outside. I was looking for something of that kind and replied that I was agreeable.

"Dick's idea was that we should use our knives and to keep to it till one was killed or he hollered 'Enough!' which neither of us would do to save his life. I said the best plan would be to use our fists. A duel with knives was liable to be over sudden, while a fist-fight would last much longer, and therefore give both more enjoyment. It wouldn't be any trouble for him as got the upper hand to pound the other to death, and being as the whole thing would be in doubt till it was over, the advantage in the way of real happiness was obvious.

"After some argument Dick seed the p'int, and agreed, and we went at it. Wal, I needn't dwell on the partic'lars. Dick put up a stiff fight, and might have give me a good deal of trouble if it hadn't been that he was weakened by whiskey, while I had long got rid of the effects of the last drop. He had to knock under, and when he found the only way to save himself was to yell 'Enough!' he done it, though, as I said, he would have held out if he had been using knives.

"I rested from pummeling him, but told him he couldn't get up till he had told the Lord what a mean scamp he was and had asked His forgiveness and promised to try to live a Christian. Dick wasn't expecting anything like that, and he b'iled over with rage. But it did no good, and I banged him agin, good and hard, and told him I never would stop till he knocked under.

"I had to soothe him a good while before he give in. He said he would do as I wished and then I let him up. He wanted to wait till night, but I wouldn't allow it, and he went down on his knees and sailed in. I made him pray out loud, so as to be sure he put things in right shape. Now, Deerfoot, tell me whether I managed *that* job right."

The Shawanoe was puzzled, for the trapper had submitted a new phase of the most interesting question to him. But Deerfoot was shrewd.

"Let my brother finish his story."

"Oh, the job came out all right. Dick was sulky and ugly for a few days, though I made him stick to his prayers every morning and night. But bye and bye, when the whiskey got out of him, he begun to improve. One day he laughed, but was so scared by it that he didn't speak till night. Soon after that he told me he felt a good deal better, which the same I replied was because he was getting over the long drunk he had been on for a dozen years.

"Wal, Dick continued to improve. His spirits rose, his appetite was stronger, he could stand more work, and I noticed that in praying he yelled louder than ever.

All these was good signs and showed that I had managed the bus'ness right, so I won't ask your opinion on my style, Deerfoot.

"Then Dick told me of the job that French Pete and him had put up on me. I could afford to laugh, but Dick was that mad that he was eager to get back to St. Louis, so that he could go down to Pete's place and smash things as I done. But I talked him out of that, and he promised me he wouldn't undertake the bus'ness till I could jine him. You know there's a sweetness about such work that I 'spose made me selfish. I warn't willing he should have all the enj'yment to himself.

"I've showed my faith in Dick by sending him home with the peltries. You see it isn't like a chap trying to make a man of himself when the temptation is at his elbow. Dick had to go without for months, and that give him enough time to become master of himself. All that I'm afeard of is that he'll get impatient when he catches sight of French Pete's place and forget his promise to me."

CHAPTER XXVII.
"GOOD-BYE."

The remainder of the homeward journey was without special incident. It was several days before Victor Shelton fully recovered from the pounding caused by his fall into the torrent. The loss of his rifle was keenly felt, but he did not fret, for it would have been ungrateful after his marvelous escape.

Jack Halloway's spirits were irrepressible, and his good nature was like so much sunshine. The only fault to be found with him was his inclination to burst into song, without waiting for urging on the part of his friends. He was gifted with a tremendous voice, but unfortunately he had no more idea of a tune than a grizzly bear. But no one could criticize the fellow, who was the life of the little party.

The course of our friends was southeast, leading through the present States of Wyoming, Colorado and into Kansas, where they struck the trail of the year before. This was followed across Missouri, and, without mishap, all four reached in due time that old French town on the Mississippi.

Deerfoot and the boys stayed there for one night and a part of a day. It was a visit which they always remembered. The only fly in the ointment was the discovery by Jack Halloway that Dick Burley, after all, had broken his promise. He had not been in St. Louis twenty-four hours when he sauntered down to French Pete's place. That worthy met him with a grin, supposing he had come to make his report, whose nature was not doubted. Then Dick, after denouncing the fellow as he deserved, proceeded to business in as emphatic a fashion as Jack had done the preceding year. He was equally thorough, perhaps more so, for he not only left the place a wreck, and the proprietor senseless, but "laid out" two brawlers who happened to be present and were imprudent enough to try to help the landlord.

"I've one hope," said Jack, in telling of the incident. "Pete will start up agin and then it'll be *my* turn to make a friendly call on him."

In that humble home, on the upper margin of the straggling town of St. Louis, Jack Halloway introduced George and Victor Shelton and Deerfoot to his mother. She was a sprightly little lady, who could not have weighed a hundred pounds, and whose soft, wavy, white hair and pink cheeks and regular features spoke of the unusual beauty that was hers when she was the belle of the town. She had a serene beauty and winsomeness that warmed the hearts of the callers from the moment they first saw her.

As soon as the introductions and greetings were over, Jack caught his mother in his arms and tossed her as high as the ceiling would permit, catching her as she descended and kissing her as if she were a little child. Then, waving the others to seats, he dropped into the single rocking chair and held her on his knee during the conversation that followed. Her soul was wrapped up in this massive boy with the strength of a giant, and her happiness over his restoration to her after her years of prayer had a pathos and sweetness that nothing else in all the world could give.

When the chatter had gone on for a few minutes Jack drew his mother's face down beside his own and whispered:

"Did you ever see as handsome a chap as that young Indian sitting over there in the corner? Look how modest he is, as if he didn't wish to be noticed. Didn't you remember, when I told you his name is Deerfoot, that he's the chap that made me throw away my flask of whiskey and was the cause of my becoming a *man*?"

"No," replied the astonished parent, "I didn't recall it. I must have a talk with him before he leaves us."

It was arranged after supper that George and Victor should go to the home of Dick Burley to sleep. Room could have been made for them in the cabin of Jack Halloway by letting the three rest on the floor, and he and his mother would have been pleased; but the brothers showed good taste by accepting the invitation of Burley, at whose house, for the first time in many months, they slept in a bed. There was happy content in that home also, for what loving, devoted wife is not thankful when her husband is restored to her and is in his right mind?

That humble home where Jack Halloway smoked his pipe, with his mother knitting beside him and Deerfoot a little way off in his chair, was the picture of serene, grateful pleasure on the cool summer night, long ago, when the three sat in converse.

The youth was so drawn to the pure, sweet-faced, motherly lady that he could not refuse her request to tell her about himself. He talked more freely than was his wont, and said many things he would not have said in the presence of others. She penetrated the nobility of the youth, who could read and write well, whose mind was stored with considerable knowledge, whose woodcraft approached as near perfection as mortal man can attain, and whose strength, skill and prowess (as she gathered from incidents brought out in the course of the evening) were the superior of any person's whom she had ever seen. In addition, as she said to her son the next day, anyone would be tempted to talk to Deerfoot, because it was such a pleasure to look upon the handsome countenance and to make him smile and show his beautiful teeth.

So it was that Deerfoot was compelled to tell the whole story of his encounter with Taggarak, with its remarkable sequel; of his fight with the grizzly bear, and his conquest of Whirlwind, the peerless stallion. He never would have done this but for the persistent questioning of Mrs. Halloway. The boys had told Jack enough on the long ride from the mountains to St. Louis for him to give his mother the necessary pointers, and he helped her in driving the Shawanoe into a corner, where he could not otherwise extricate himself.

The wonderful thing in the estimation of the good woman was that the hero of these and many other exploits was a *Christian.* She had never seen one of his race who professed to be a follower of the Meek and Lowly One, though she had heard of such from the missionaries; but she agreed with her son that no more perfect exemplar of Christianity was to be found anywhere.

On the morrow, when the time came to part, Mrs. Halloway took the hand of Deerfoot in her dainty palm, and in a trembling voice thanked him for what he had done for her through what he did for her son. She promised to pray for him every day of her remaining life, and while he stood trying to keep back the tears she added:

"Please bend your head a little."

He bent down and she touched her lips to his forehead, and, still holding the hand, said so that all, Jack, the Shelton boys and Dick Burley, could hear, as they gathered round to say the parting words:

"Well done, good and faithful servant!"

The benison thus bestowed remained with Deerfoot all the way home and to the end of his life. In the cool depths of the forest, amid the fragrance of brown leaves, the bark of trees and of bursting bud and blossom, and by the flow of the crystal brook, he heard the gentle whisper. It came to him when the snow sifted against his frame and the bite of the Arctic blast was as merciless as the fangs of the she-wolf. Above the crash of the hurricane that uprooted and splintered the century-old monarchs of the woods the words rang out like the notes of an angel's trumpet, and in the watches of the night, under the star-gleam or in the fleecy moonlight, while stillness brooded over a sleeping world, the music swung back and forth like a censer through the corridors of the soul, with a sweetness that told him the strings of the harp throbbed under the touch of the fingers of God himself.

CHAPTER XXVIII.
RETROSPECT.[2]

"I am the son and only child of Taggarak, a leading war chief for many years of the Blackfoot Indians. I had an elder brother, but he died before reaching manhood. I remember the visit made by Deerfoot the Shawanoe to our tribe, in the autumn and winter of 1804 and 1805. He came from Ohio, in company with two brothers named Shelton, that were white, and with Mul-tal-la, who belonged to our own people, and had made the journey eastward into the Shawanoe country. Mul-tal-la had a companion when he left us, but he was accidentally killed after arriving in the East.

"I was not quite five years old when I first saw Deerfoot and his two friends, yet I can never forget him, for he was the most remarkable youth, white or red, that I ever met."

(Here follows a description of Deerfoot's appearance, his traits, his skill with rifle and bow, his athletic prowess and his unequaled woodcraft. This need not be repeated, since you are familiar with it. The statement which follows, however, is one of the most remarkable ever penned.)

"I was in the Big Lodge on the afternoon Deerfoot spoke to many of our people of the white man's God, who, he said, was the God of the red man as well. Young as I was, I stood at the knee of my mother, thrilled and almost breathless under the spell of the simple eloquence of the Shawanoe, many of whose words I remember. In the midst of his address my father, Chief Taggarak, strode into the lodge. He passed so close to me that his knee brushed my shoulder. My mother and I looked up at him, but he did not see us, nor did he notice anyone except Deerfoot. His eyes were fixed on the young Shawanoe, and we all thought he meant to attack him.

"Deerfoot saw him enter, stopped speaking and looked steadily at the chief as he drew near. Deerfoot always carried his knife at his girdle, though of course he had laid aside his gun. I remember wondering why he did not draw his weapon, but, instead of doing so, he placed his hands behind his back and calmly surveyed Taggarak, without the least sign of fear. From what I afterward learned, I am sure that if my father had attacked the Shawanoe, the chief would have been quickly overcome, if not killed.

"Within two paces of Deerfoot, Taggarak wheeled about, *faced* his people and made an impassioned avowal of his belief in the Christian religion. He declared that the true God had spoken to him when he tried to hide himself in the woods and to close his ears against His words. That God had not allowed him to sleep or eat or drink or rest till he threw himself on his face, and with streaming eyes begged Him to forgive and take him into His favor.

"Never was there such excitement among the Blackfoot tribe as was caused by the declaration of their greatest war chief that he had become a Christian. It almost rent the tribe in twain. We had a number of villages and different chiefs, but Taggarak was the greatest of them all.

"It was clear to everyone that he looked upon Deerfoot the Shawanoe as more than an ordinary human being. In truth I thought and still think the same, and I believe you will agree with me when you hear the rest of my story. Taggarak asked Deerfoot whether he should give up his chieftaincy, and was ready to do whatever the Shawanoe advised. Deerfoot told him to remain chief as long as he lived, but to be merciful to his enemies, never to fight except in defence of his home and people, and to pray to God morning and night and to do all he could to please Him in his actions, his words and his thoughts. Deerfoot did much in the way of teaching him, and Taggarak became a Christian, as did my mother and myself and others of our tribe, though I never understood all the height and depth and breadth of God's love and plans until I had grown to manhood and talked with the missionaries.

"Christianity would have been firmly planted among my people but for the acts of the white men themselves. When the expedition of Lewis and Clark came through our country one of them killed a Blackfoot. No doubt there was some justification for the act, but it made our tribe the enemies of the white men, and many who professed to love the God of the palefaces now cast away such love and would have none of it. Taggarak was much grieved and indignant over the action of the white men, but nothing could weaken or shake his faith in Christianity."

(The incident alluded to occurred July 27, 1806. A party of Blackfeet stole a number of horses belonging to Lewis and Clark's party, were pursued, and one of the Indians killed and another wounded. The tribe was so embittered toward the whites that they were treacherous enemies to them for many years afterward.)

"From the year following this sad event, however, the authority of Taggarak waned. He did not care for power, and was content to let it slip gradually from him and pass to others. I could have become chief had I wished it, but I knew I was distrusted because I professed Christianity, and the Blackfeet and I thought so differently about everything that I remained a simple warrior, content to serve my father and mother, as an obedient son.

"I did not know for years of the encounter between Taggarak and Deerfoot in the wood, when the chief sought his life, but was overcome and then spared by the Shawanoe. Deerfoot never spoke of it, and I was almost grown when my father told my mother and me of the strange incident, which was the means of the chief's accepting the religion that the youth taught by word and example.

"When Deerfoot left our village, Taggarak begged him to visit him again. He urged so hard that the youth said he would do so if he could, but he saw little hope and thought their next meeting would have to wait till both passed into the hunting grounds above.

"Taggarak meditated much over the coming of Deerfoot. As he grew older he often went to the elevation, a little way from our village, and near where he had been overcome by the Shawanoe, and passed hours gazing toward the East, looking and hoping for sight of the youth who did not come. He always went alone to the spot and did not suspect his action was noticed by anyone. But at the request of my mother, I stealthily followed the chief. He seated himself on a broad, flat rock, which gave him a view of many miles of mountain, wood and stream, and it seemed that for the hour I watched him he never took his gaze from the point in the sky where the sun first showed itself. I have sometimes wondered whether my father mistook any approaching warrior for the Shawanoe. I never learned, for not once did he ever refer to those lonely visits to the elevation.

"One day my father said, with his old sternness of manner, that since Deerfoot was not coming to see him, I must take a message to the Shawanoe in his distant home. It was a startling command, but was not unwelcome to me. I had heard much of the white man's country, and knew the palefaces were fast pushing into our own. I had listened to Mul-tal-la's wonderful stories times without number, and often resolved that when an opportunity came I should visit the white towns and settlements.

"I was glad, therefore, when my father spoke as he did, and still more glad when Mul-tal-la, although he had a wife and two children, offered to go with me. He was anxious to see Deerfoot and the acquaintances he had made many years before, whose memory was always a pleasure to him.

"My father's message to the Shawanoe amounted to little. I was to tell him the chief was still true to his faith, and to ask him whether he could come to the chief, and, if he could not, whether he still remembered Taggarak. That was all.

"I was a grown man when, with Mul-tal-la as my companion, I rode down from the Blackfoot country and we set out on the long journey he had made more than twenty years before. He remembered every river, stream, mountain and prairie, though the settlements had brought many changes, and on the way to the Ohio he met several acquaintances.

"It would be of no interest to tell of our journey, though we had more than one adventure. The first place we visited was the little town of Woodvale, so familiar to Mul-tal-la, and which had grown to that extent that it had taken a new name.

"There we found George and Victor Shelton, almost in middle life, both married and among the leading citizens. They were filled with joy to see Mul-tal-la, and did all they could to make our visit pleasant. But we had talked only a little while when we were grieved to learn that Deerfoot, who had moved to the west of the Mississippi, had been dead a good many years. Not only that, but the manner of his death was the saddest of which I had ever heard. (See "The Last War Trail.")

"We stayed for several weeks in Ohio and met many old friends of the Shawanoe. The one whom I best remember was Simon Kenton, who had great fame as a hunter, and who had always been a close comrade of Deerfoot. He was an old man when I saw him, but as strong and active as many who had lived only half his years. He came to Woodvale the night before we left on our return and stayed with Victor Shelton. His eyes filled with tears when he spoke of Deerfoot, and said that the memory of the brave, blameless life he lived in all circumstances had more to do with making Kenton himself a Christian than did the camp meeting at which he professed conversion.

"Well, we set out for home, and though a part of the journey was made in winter we met with no mishap. When we arrived, Mul-tal-la went straight to his lodge to see his wife and children and I hurried to my home, where I knew the chief had long expected me. I was greatly relieved to find him and my mother well.

"When I came into my father's presence, and before I had time to do more than speak my pleasure, he raised his hand as a command for me to keep silent.

"'I know what you would say, but you need not tell me. Deerfoot has been here and told me all.'

"'But Deerfoot is dead,' I replied; 'that cannot be.'

"'Did I not say he has visited me since you were gone, and told me all?'

"And then, forbidding me to open my lips, he related the full story of Deerfoot's death. He gave the particulars, and was not wrong in the slightest one. The chief need not have forbidden me to speak, for I could not say a word for a long time afterward. He told me nothing more. I cannot explain it."

(Possibly psychologists may find the explanation of this remarkable fact in mental telepathy, but how shall we explain the still more extraordinary statement that follows?)

"My mother had grown old and feeble and died a few months after I came home. I noticed that father stopped going to the elevation beyond the village and looking toward the rising sun for the coming of Deerfoot. Nor did he seem to wish to speak of him, though I know the Shawanoe was much in his thoughts. The chief gradually failed, and when the weather grew cold he did not leave his lodge.

"He and I lived together. I gave him affectionate attention and did not let him lack for comfort. Others often visited him, for the Blackfeet could not forget that he had been one of their greatest war chiefs. Our lodge was not fashioned like the others. One side was the face of a large rock, against which we always kindled the fire. At each of the opposite two corners was a strong post. These were connected at the tops by a horizontal beam and from each post was stretched another beam, whose farther end rested on the rock. This and the three beams gave support for the framework of the roof, which was made of the boughs of trees. The sides and walls were of thick bark lined with buffalo robes. This made the square room below free of all supports or posts. My bed of furs was at one side and that of my father opposite. An opening in the roof, where it joined the rock and exactly over the fire, gave an outlet for the smoke.

"One calm, cold night in autumn, after I had piled a deal of wood on the blaze and seen that my father was warmly wrapped in furs and sleeping comfortably, I lay down and fell asleep almost at once. It could not have been long afterward that I was awakened by the sound of people talking together. At first I thought they were outside the lodge, but the fire was burning so bright that it was like noonday within and I saw that the two persons who were conversing were standing only a few paces from me.

"One was Chief Taggarak, my father. His face was turned partly away and toward me and there could be no mistake as to him. The other's back and one shoulder hid his features, but something familiar in his appearance and the sound of his voice struck me. While I was looking and listening he shifted his position and I saw his face.

"*It was Deerfoot the Shawanoe!*

"It Was Deerfoot, The Shawanoe."

"No one who had ever seen that Indian youth could possibly make an error. I never looked upon such comely features or such a graceful form, nor did I ever listen to so musical a voice. Like a person in a dream, I felt no special surprise at seeing before me a person who had died years before.

"I studied him from head to foot. One of the first things I noticed was that the stained eagle feathers, which he always used to wear in his hair, were not there, nor did he have his knife at his girdle nor was his rifle in his hand. I don't suppose they have need of such things in heaven.

"During this talk between Deerfoot and my father I did not speak or rise to my feet. I expected the Shawanoe to say something to me and I had no wish to break in upon the talk. They spent ten or fifteen minutes thus, and then Deerfoot took the hand of my father, pressed it warmly and turned to go. As he did so, he seemed for the first time to see me. He stopped, looked down, smiled and uttered my name. Then he checked himself, walked to the corner of the lodge, drew aside the buffalo robe which served as a door and passed out into the night.

"My father stood for a minute looking after him, and then, with a glowing face, turned to me:

"'Did you see him?'

"'I did, and heard his voice.'

"'You lost nothing of what he said to me?'

"'Not a word.'

"'Tell them to no one. Now sleep.'

"It was a long time before I closed my eyes, and when I did so the wonderful words that had fallen from the lips of Deerfoot were in my ears. To me the strangest part of this strange experience is that which followed. When morning came I found I could not remember a syllable that the Shawanoe had said. I spoke to my father, and he talked of the visit of Deerfoot as he would have talked of the visit of one of our own Blackfeet. I told him I had forgotten the Shawanoe's words and asked him to tell them to me again. He replied that God did not wish me to remember them and he denied my request, which I respected him too much ever to repeat.

"Chief Taggarak lived several years longer. I have tried many times to recall the words spoken by Deerfoot when he visited my father, but I have never succeeded in bringing back a single one of them."

Made in the USA
Monee, IL
19 April 2022